Unpacked

How to Detach From The Subconscious Beliefs
That Are Sabotaging Your Life

KRISTEN JACOBSEN, LCPC

Disclaimers

Portions of this book are works of fiction. Any references to historical events, real people, or real places are used fictitiously. Other names, characters, places, and events are products of the author's imagination, and any resemblances to actual events, places, or persons, living or dead, is entirely coincidental.

Portions of this book are works of nonfiction. Certain names and identifying characteristics have been changed.

ISBN: 979-8-89694-336-5 - Paperback
ISBN: 979-8-89694-335-8 - Ebook
ISBN: 979-8-89694-337-2 - Hardcover

First Edition
Published in the United States of America

For more information, visit: https://bio.site/kristenjacobsen

This book is dedicated to my parents.

Two imperfect humans, doing the best they could, given their circumstances, with the resources they had available to them at the time. I love you both.

To help you get the most out of this book, I'm giving you the first exercise from the accompanying workbook—completely FREE. This workbook expands on the concepts in these pages, guiding you through deeper exercises designed to create real, lasting change. Scan the QR code to grab your freebie and start exploring your own patterns and beliefs!

Scan Me!

CONTENTS

INTRODUCTION

"I am not what happens to me. I choose who I become." - *Carl Jung*

We've all had those moments—experiences that leave an emotional mark, whether we like it or not. They may not always be the kind of experiences you'd label as "trauma," but make no mistake: they shape who we are. These moments help form core beliefs about ourselves, other people, and the world. And if you're reading this, there's a good chance you have some unfinished business from your past, and it's still messing with you in adulthood. Don't worry—you're not alone.

When I use the term "impactful experiences," I'm talking about anything that sticks with you. Maybe it was harsh criticism that hit a little too close to home or emotional rejection that made you feel invisible. You don't need to slap a "trauma" label on it to acknowledge its impact. What really matters is recognizing how those experiences shaped the way you think and act today.

Focusing on how these moments affected you, rather than what you call them, is where the real work begins. Maybe you're stuck with the belief that you're not good enough, or you've got some serious trust issues. Chances are, those beliefs didn't come out of nowhere. They were shaped by key moments in your past. Once you start connecting the dots, you'll see how those old experiences are still running the show. Guess what? You don't have to let them.

Let me tell you a story. Imagine someone who went through a scary accident as a kid. Most people would think that a near-death experience would be their biggest trauma, right? Not necessarily. What actually stuck with them was something completely different. It was the day their mom, drowning in financial stress, turned to them for emotional support. That's the moment that hit hardest—because suddenly, they weren't just a kid anymore. They were carrying adult-sized burdens.

Fast forward to adulthood, and sure, they remember the accident, but the thing that really gets them? It's the constant pressure to be the reliable one. That moment when they stepped up for their mom left a lasting impression: their worth became tied to being the strong one for everyone else. And that belief? It's shaped their entire outlook on life. Funny how sometimes it's not the big, obvious moments but the quiet, personal ones that do the most damage.

At the end of the day, whether you call it trauma or simply "one of those moments," the point is the same—it impacted you. The goal isn't to get stuck on labels; it's to understand how those moments shaped your beliefs and behaviors. Once you see that connection, you can finally start making changes. You can stop living out those old, outdated patterns and build something better—a healthier, more balanced version of yourself.

Our minds have an incredible ability to imagine, create, and turn ideas into reality. Every thought, belief, or vision we accept as true has the power to shape the world we experience.

Once something feels real in our minds, it naturally influences our actions, pulling us into alignment with that "reality." And this alignment doesn't just change how we feel internally—it ripples outward, shaping the environment around us to reflect and reinforce those beliefs.

When our actions and beliefs are in sync, life feels like it flows. But when they're out of alignment—when our circumstances or choices contradict those beliefs we've accepted—it creates resistance. That friction causes us distress, and it's a signal. It's pointing to a disconnect between how we see ourselves, the world, or both. It's a clue that somewhere, we've internalized a belief or perspective that's out of step with reality or with our deeper selves.

The good news? We can address this misalignment. By identifying where our beliefs no longer serve us, we can shift our perspective, recalibrate our actions, and realign with a clearer, more authentic truth. The result isn't just less struggle—it's a life that feels more honest, more fulfilling, and more aligned with who we truly are.

Impactful experiences aren't just about what happens to us—they're about the meaning we attach to them. They shape how we see control, worth, responsibility, and survival. At their core, these experiences are closely tied to the state of our nervous system and our perception of safety. Often, they're lessons we internalize in childhood, reinforced over time. To adapt, we develop coping strategies that might help us survive in the moment but lead to misalignment or self-sabotage later in life. All of these strategies have a common goal, and that's to make us feel safe.

Here's the twist: many of these behaviors—like people-pleasing, overachieving, or perfectionism—are celebrated by society. They're praised as strengths, even "superpowers," giving us external validation that makes the cycle even harder to break. The very patterns that keep us stuck are the ones we're rewarded for, making it all the more challenging to recognize what's truly driving them—and to let them go.

My Back Story

I was born in the suburbs of Philly as the eldest of four, with three younger brothers—one of whom is a half-brother. On the surface, my childhood looked pretty great: an upper-middle-class family going through the usual ups and downs, sibling rivalry, a familiar suburban routine, and family vacations at the Jersey Shore. But underneath it all, there were deeper emotional dynamics and tensions that shaped how I viewed myself and the world around me.

I want to be clear that I'm intentionally keeping things vague to avoid embarrassing or calling out anyone in my life. My relationships with family & friends are still intact, and it's important to me to protect those. My goal is not to assign blame, but to reflect on how my *own* perceptions and interpretations of the people and environments around me during childhood and adolescence shaped the beliefs I carried into adulthood. Blame has become especially irrelevant and unproductive since becoming a parent myself; however it brought a lot more to the surface.

I truly believe *most* parents did the best they could with the emotional resources and capabilities they had at the time, but there is often a misalignment between these and the needs of their child. Acceptance of the parent you had versus the parent you wanted or needed is a hard thing to reconcile later in life. Healing isn't about turning your back on your family—it's about finding your way back to yourself.

As a kid, I was surrounded by emotional immaturity, codependency, and narcissism (a result of generational trauma) which created a lot of inner turmoil for me. Relationships I once believed to be unshakable began to fall apart before my eyes. I watched multiple marriages and divorces unfold (yes, multiple) and rode the emotional rollercoaster of betrayal, infidelity, and conflict avoidance.

Anxiety and depression became regular companions, and after my parents' divorce, I developed Obsessive-Compulsive Disorder. It showed up in ways like a fear of contamination, leading me to wash my hands multiple times a day or turn off light switches with my elbows to avoid another round of handwashing. Even taking an odd number of steps in a room would set off the compulsion to retrace them to make things "even."

I learned early on that some needs go unmet, that silence could be safer than speaking up, and that trust was fragile, if not entirely elusive. Whether consciously or not, these lessons became the foundation of my core beliefs—beliefs that, at first, I didn't even realize I was forming. I internalized the ideas that my needs weren't important, that I couldn't rely on others, and perhaps most painfully, that what I had to say wasn't valued or understood.

That subconscious self-doubt only deepened when the authority figures in my life echoed it back to me. My high school guidance counselor flat-out told me I wouldn't get into

Vanderbilt University - only for me to prove him wrong. Years later, in graduate school, my advisor suggested I reconsider becoming a therapist, questioning whether it was the right path for me. Their doubt reinforced my own, making me wonder if I was truly capable or just fooling myself. And yet, despite their skepticism—and my own—I not only succeeded, but I've surpassed both of them in my career. Looking back, I realize their words didn't define me, but for a long time, I let them.

On top of that, I was hypersensitive about coming across as arrogant or conceited, so I would often keep myself small and downplay any positive traits or accomplishments. These beliefs, though rooted in childhood, followed me into adulthood via my subconscious—always present, always influencing the decisions I made and the relationships I tried to build.

Later in life, my anxious attachment style led me into my own codependent relationships, where I lost my sense of self. Alcohol became part of the equation too, blurring the line between healthy coping and unhealthy escape. And through it all, I kept asking myself the same question: why was I stuck in these same emotional patterns, unable to move forward?

It wasn't until I really started looking at the beliefs I had formed—beliefs rooted in my formative years—that I began to understand how I was sabotaging my own life. By thinking my needs didn't matter, I stopped asking for what I wanted. By believing I couldn't trust others, I pulled back emotionally and expected the worst. And by convincing myself that my voice lacked value, I stayed silent when I should have spoken up.

Things began to shift when I stopped seeking approval from my parents, teachers, and supervisors. For the first time, I wasn't trying to make anyone proud—I was proud of myself. It was a quiet but powerful change, a sense of self-confidence that felt like I was finally stepping into who I was meant to be. External validation became just that—a bonus, not something I needed to feel worthy. That inner shift gave me a sense of freedom and control over my life that I had never experienced before.

Where I Am Today

I'm now married with two kids, and after a lot of inner work, I've developed a pretty solid secure attachment style. I have no issue asserting my needs - probably more than my husband would like. People-pleasing? That's a thing of the past, and I'm not living in fear of making mistakes anymore. I see them as an opportunity for learning and growth. While I would still consider myself a recovering perfectionist, anxiety is no longer in the driver's seat of my life, and running a successful business has pushed me to really find my voice and set boundaries, even when it makes me uncomfortable. If I can get here, believe me - you can too.

The road to unraveling these beliefs has been long and winding, filled with moments of clarity and continued struggle. But it's a journey I believe many of us find ourselves on—whether we realize it or not. This book isn't just my story; it's a reflection of how we all develop beliefs that shape us, sometimes to our detriment, and how the process of unlearning those beliefs can open the door to tremendous healing and growth.

Most of what our brain processes doesn't come from the outside world—it comes from within. Our thoughts, perceptions, and beliefs shape how we see and experience life. Only a small part of what we take in comes from actual events around us.

Everything else is filtered through our personal lens, shaped by past experiences and emotions.

This filter tends to confirm the beliefs we already hold, especially the deep-rooted core beliefs about ourselves. For instance, if you believe deep down that you're not good enough, your brain will look for evidence to prove it. You might overlook compliments or positive experiences and zero in on anything that feels like criticism or failure, which only reinforces that belief further.

Think of core beliefs like a pair of sunglasses: each person's lenses are tinted a little differently, affecting how they see things. For many, those "shades" are tinted by negative beliefs, leading to harmful patterns. They only let us see things that align with our internal story. This creates a cycle where we keep finding proof of what we already believe, whether it's true or not. The only way to break that cycle is by paying attention to how we're interpreting things and asking ourselves: Is this really accurate, or is it just a reflection of what I expect to see? When we do this, we can start challenging old beliefs and see things in a clearer, more balanced way. The first step in changing those negative beliefs is identifying them—and that's exactly what this book is here to help you do.

Core beliefs are rarely the result of a single moment; instead, they take shape through a series of experiences that consistently reinforce a developing idea about ourselves or the world. Each time we experience something that supports this belief—whether it's feeling ignored, criticized, or unworthy—it adds another layer, gradually making the belief more ingrained. As I mentioned earlier, we naturally seek out evidence that confirms our existing beliefs, so when these moments keep validating negative ideas, they begin to feel like undeniable truths. The more these experiences accumulate, the stronger and more deeply rooted the belief becomes, shaping our view of ourselves and the world in a way that can be hard to untangle without conscious effort.

Who This Book Is For

This book is for anyone looking for self-awareness and change. Whether you've been on this journey for years or are just starting to ask deeper questions, this book will guide you in reflecting on your past, understanding your core beliefs, and moving forward with greater clarity and intention.

If you've ever felt that your needs aren't important, that you can't trust others, or that your voice isn't valued, you may be carrying beliefs from the past that have impacted your choices and relationships. These beliefs often develop as protective mechanisms, helping us navigate difficult experiences in childhood. But as we grow into adulthood, they can turn into limiting patterns that affect our well-being, happiness, and ability to connect with others. This book is for anyone prepared to examine those patterns and challenge the ways they may be holding you back.

We tend to think we react directly to events, but every situation first passes through our subconscious. This layer, packed with past beliefs and experiences, filters how we interpret and respond. For example, if someone ignores you in a conversation, it might trigger a belief like "I'm not important," which then leads to sadness or frustration. Your emotions guide your actions—whether that's shutting down or lashing out. It's not the event but the belief driving your reaction.

Our subconscious moves fast but doesn't always get things right. Imagine a caveman who sees a bear for the first time— he's not scared until he sees it attack someone. From then on, he associates bears with danger. The same goes for everyday stress. Maybe your anxiety stems from an old experience where you felt like a failure, and now that feeling resurfaces in new situations. The emotions are real, but the beliefs behind them might not be.

Let's say as a kid you were criticized for making mistakes. Now, when faced with a challenge at work, you feel stress. It's not the task causing that stress, but a belief you're not capable. By tracing these feelings back, you can start asking why they exist. If the answer is "I'm going to fail," dig deeper—"Why do I think that?" The root might be "I'm not capable." Once you identify the belief, start questioning it. Have you succeeded before? Can you gather proof against that belief? This process rewires your brain over time.

The tricky part is that our subconscious treats these beliefs as absolute truths, especially when they form in childhood. These beliefs become so ingrained that we don't even realize they drive our actions and emotions. If left unchecked, they keep creating stress and anxiety in our lives. To shift these beliefs, you need to interrupt the cycle.

Sometimes, we even feel bad for feeling bad, adding another layer of self-judgment. But emotions are valid. What you need to question are the thoughts behind them. And if you've been through trauma or emotional neglect, it's important to remember that what happened wasn't your fault. Childhood often teaches us to give up parts of ourselves for approval, leading to deep wounds. But those wounds can heal.

Emotional pain doesn't require extreme trauma to exist. Even childhood experiences in which your feelings were consistently dismissed can lead to anxiety, depression, or stress. Many people downplay their struggles, thinking they "shouldn't" be this upset, but everyone's experience is valid. Your subconscious has been trying to protect you, but it's time to teach it that you deserve more than survival—you deserve to thrive. The journey is tough, but as Carl Jung said, "What we do not make conscious emerges later as fate."

This book isn't about blaming our parents or caregivers. Kids don't internalize their parents' intentions, they internalize how it made them *feel*. Childhood is complex, and while our experiences shape us, this book focuses on *our own interpretations and perceptions* of those experiences. These personal lenses form the core beliefs that influence us, and this is where we have the power to make meaningful change. This process is about understanding, not blame—it's about acknowledging how we've been shaped and deciding how we want to move forward. Not everyone will see things the same way, and that's perfectly fine. This book is about diving into your own self-perception and understanding the role it's played in your life.

Through practical exercises, real-life stories, and reflective prompts, this book helps you develop the awareness needed to address patterns of behavior that may be holding you back *(please note this is not to be considered therapy)*. By identifying your core beliefs and understanding how they were formed, you can begin to challenge their validity and make choices that align with your true values and goals. This book is for those who want to reclaim their sense of worth, rediscover their voice, and take concrete steps toward personal growth.

What to Expect

This book is the result of my experiences as both a therapist and human being. The case studies in this book are drawn from the hundreds of real clients I've worked with over my 15+ years as a licensed psychotherapist. While the stories reflect genuine experiences and challenges, all names and identifying details have been changed to maintain confidentiality and protect personal privacy. Any resemblance to an actual person is purely coincidental. My clients often come to me for help with anxiety, only to realize that unresolved issues from their past are still shaping their present lives - those hidden blind spots we all have. These case studies dive deep into the transformational work they've done, offering insight into how awareness of these blind spots can reveal hidden patterns and lead to lasting change.

The goal of this book isn't just to offer insights but to guide you through your own process of self-awareness and introspection. As you move through the chapters, you'll be encouraged to explore the beliefs that have shaped your life since childhood, and see how they've influenced your decisions, relationships, and sense of self. By gaining clarity around these core beliefs, you'll better understand how they've impacted your adult life—and how you can begin to reshape them.

You may have struggled with feelings of inadequacy, chosen relationships that mirror old patterns, or avoided opportunities because a part of you still believes you're not good enough. By the end of this journey, you'll have a clearer understanding of how these beliefs formed, and how they've been limiting you. The insights you gain will help you identify when these beliefs surface and challenge them, rather than unconsciously following them.

This book doesn't stop at self-awareness. It provides practical tools and exercises to help you make meaningful changes. You'll learn to rewrite the narrative that has shaped your life for too long and replace it with a healthier, more adaptive one that reflects who you are now—not the person you were as a child trying to navigate a difficult world. These exercises will help you integrate what you've learned into real, tangible changes in your life.

By the end of the book, you'll not only have a deeper understanding of yourself, but you'll also have the tools to break the patterns that have limited you. While core beliefs shape your life, you have the power to reshape them. Through this process of introspection and self-awareness, you'll gain the tools needed to move forward as a more empowered version of yourself, free from the self-sabotaging tendencies that have held you back.

What's at Stake

If you choose not to take a deeper look at your core beliefs and how they may be shaping your life, you risk staying trapped in destructive cycles of self-sabotage. If you're not ready, that's okay—just keep this book handy until you are. These patterns may feel so natural that they go unnoticed, manifesting as ways of coping that keep you stuck. Whether it's intellectualizing your emotions instead of processing them, doom scrolling to avoid your thoughts, or turning to alcohol, drugs, or overeating to numb discomfort—all are forms of self-sabotage. While they might offer temporary relief, they reinforce feelings of inadequacy and low self-worth, leaving you more disconnected from yourself.

Self-sabotage can also show up in behaviors that seem productive but are actually distractions from deeper issues. You might throw yourself into excessive cleaning, working long hours, or over-exercising—anything to stay busy and avoid facing underlying emotions or beliefs. Perfectionism, with its impossible standards, keeps you chasing approval while reinforcing the idea that you're never good enough. Isolating from relationships, whether out of fear or self-protection, can lead to deep loneliness.

Another risk of ignoring core beliefs is falling into a routine of harsh self-criticism. You might engage in negative self-talk, blaming yourself for not being "better" or feeling there's something inherently wrong with you. Alternatively, you may blame others for your unhappiness, avoiding personal responsibility for change. Over time, these behaviors erode your self-worth, leaving you stuck in a cycle of frustration and discontent. You might withdraw from meaningful connections or use sleep as an escape, only to wake up with the same sense of emptiness.

These self-sabotaging behaviors chip away at your potential. You might see glimpses of the life you want but feel unable to reach it, held back by the beliefs and habits that seemingly protect you. But those beliefs no longer serve you, and if left unexamined, they will continue to deepen, leading to stronger feelings of inadequacy and hopelessness. You may even start to believe that lasting change is impossible.

By not addressing these beliefs, you also risk passing them on to future generations or those closest to you. Emotional withdrawal, unrealistic standards, and criticism can be internalized by others, continuing the cycle. Without realizing it, you may teach others the same harmful beliefs that have kept you stuck.

Ultimately, if you don't confront these core beliefs, you risk missing out on the life you truly want. Instead of creating a future built on self-awareness, compassion, and resilience, you may repeat the same patterns that hold you back. The stakes are high, but the power to change is within your reach. This book offers you the tools to recognize these self-sabotaging behaviors, challenge the beliefs that no longer serve you, and move toward a life of greater fulfillment and connection.

Survival Patterns

Family dysfunction isn't always the dramatic, door-slamming, shouting-match kind. More often, it's tucked into the quiet stuff—unspoken rules, invisible expectations, and the subtle ways love and approval were tied to how well you followed the script. Maybe you grew up with this nagging feeling that something wasn't right, but you couldn't quite put your finger on it. You've probably even asked yourself, *Was it really that bad?*

Here's the thing: dysfunctional family patterns don't magically vanish just because we grow up and move out. They sneak into our relationships, shape how we see ourselves, and influence how we show up in the world—usually without us even realizing it.

And no, it's not always because someone was intentionally trying to mess you up. A lot of these patterns get passed down like family heirlooms—not out of malice, but as survival strategies. In many cultures, things like loyalty, self-sacrifice, and keeping quiet are seen as the glue holding the family together. But when that glue comes at the cost of your emotional well-being, it leaves wounds that are real, even if they're hard to name.

Many of us develop habits or "survival patterns" based on these past experiences. One common pattern is being hypervigilant, where you're overly tuned into others' emotions, constantly on edge trying to anticipate shifts in their moods. This often stems from growing up in an environment where you didn't feel emotionally safe, leaving you anxious and drained from always watching for potential problems. Another pattern is struggling to set boundaries—you might find it hard to say no or protect your personal space because you want to avoid conflict or keep everyone happy, often at the expense of your own needs.

Some people fall into overgiving and caretaking, always putting others first, which can lead to burnout and frustration when your own needs aren't met. Similarly, perfectionism and overfunctioning arise when you push yourself too hard, believing you need to be perfect or in control to feel worthy. This is exhausting and often leaves you feeling unsatisfied no matter how much you do.

Another survival pattern is self-doubt, where you constantly question your decisions or look to others for approval, holding you back from living confidently. There's also the fear of conflict or abandonment, where you avoid speaking up for yourself out of fear of upsetting others or pushing them away. Lastly, internalized guilt or shame shows up as a constant feeling of blame or not being good enough, even when it's not your fault. This can eat away at your self-esteem and fuel negative thoughts about yourself.

Kelly's Story

Kelly, a 38-year-old financial analyst, had spent much of her life being overly attuned to the emotions and needs of those around her. Growing up in a household where conflict and emotional instability were common, Kelly developed a survival pattern of constantly monitoring her parents' moods to maintain peace. This hypervigilance became ingrained, and as an adult, she found herself always on edge, trying to anticipate shifts in her supervisors' and colleagues' attitudes in order to avoid conflict or criticism. Despite her success in her career, this constant emotional scanning left her feeling exhausted and anxious, making it difficult for her to focus on her own needs.

In addition to her hypervigilance, Kelly struggled with setting boundaries at work. She found it nearly impossible to say no when coworkers or managers asked for help, even if it meant taking on more tasks than she could handle. She worried that declining would upset them or damage her reputation as a team player. At home, Kelly's boundary issues continued; she often overcommitted to social or family obligations, sacrificing her personal time to avoid letting others down. These habits of overgiving and people-pleasing, rooted in her fear of conflict and rejection, left Kelly feeling drained and unappreciated, though she rarely expressed her frustration out loud.

As Kelly navigated her demanding workload, she also battled a persistent sense of self-doubt. She frequently questioned her decisions, sought validation from her peers, and hesitated to trust her own judgment. Kelly's fear of making mistakes or disappointing others fueled a cycle of overfunctioning, where she constantly overextended herself to maintain control and perfection. This fear-driven behavior ultimately left her feeling both emotionally and physically depleted, as she struggled to balance the high expectations she placed on herself with her unmet personal needs.

Kelly's hypervigilance, combined with her difficulty establishing boundaries, created a pattern of emotional burnout. She rarely allowed herself to step back or prioritize self-care, believing that her worth was tied to how well she managed others' emotions and met their expectations. This survival pattern, developed from her past experiences, continued to undermine her ability to find peace and satisfaction, leaving her trapped in a cycle of overworking and emotional depletion.

Through therapy and self-reflection, Kelly came to recognize that her constant need to anticipate others' emotions and her reluctance to set boundaries were blind spots that kept her stuck in an exhausting cycle. She began to see how these patterns, while once necessary for survival in her childhood, were no longer serving her in adulthood.

With this realization, Kelly took small but meaningful steps toward change—she started by setting clear limits at work, gradually saying no to requests that stretched her too thin, and prioritizing tasks that aligned with her values. She also learned to tolerate discomfort when others were disappointed, understanding that their reactions were not her responsibility to manage. Over time, Kelly found a newfound sense of confidence in her ability to navigate relationships without losing herself in the process. This shift allowed her to reclaim her personal time, focus on her own needs, and experience a greater sense of balance and fulfillment in both her professional and personal life.

Emotional Blind Spots

Just like a good driver knows cars have blind spots—those areas you can't see because the car blocks your view—people have emotional blind spots too. These are parts of ourselves we don't notice, but they still impact our lives. The tricky part is, while drivers are taught to check their mirrors, most of us aren't taught how to spot emotional blind spots. As a result, we can go through life unaware of them, even though they're closely tied to our core beliefs and can cause all kinds of issues.

Emotional blind spots often stem from core beliefs. For example, if you believe you're not good enough, it can lead to anxiety, depression, and conflict in relationships, without you realizing the source. These blind spots can also show up in unhealthy habits like overeating, substance abuse, or avoiding tough situations. But the good news is, once you become aware of these blind spots and the beliefs behind them, you can start to address them.

One common blind spot is intellectualizing emotions. When a child is upset, they'll say they're sad or mad. Ask an adult, and you're more likely to hear words like "upset" or "pissed off," which are less about the real emotion and more about avoiding it. To cut through this, ask yourself how a child would describe what you're feeling—it's a simple way to cut through the noise and understand what's really going on inside.

Another blind spot is trying to control emotions. We often think we can make ourselves happy when we're sad or confident when we're anxious, but forcing emotions away only makes them stronger. The key is accepting them as they are—uncomfortable, but not dangerous. Once we stop fighting our emotions, we can focus on what we actually can control, like how we respond or what we do next.

Lastly, we often judge ourselves for how we feel, which only makes things worse. We tell ourselves we shouldn't be angry, or that feeling sad is weak. But emotions aren't something we can control, so there's no point in beating ourselves up over them. When we stop judging ourselves, painful emotions tend to fade faster. By recognizing these blind spots, we can better understand our emotions and feel more in control of our lives.

Emotions are powerful messengers—not good or bad, just signals meant to guide and inform us. They offer a window into our inner world, often highlighting unmet needs, unresolved experiences, or deeply held values. When certain emotions keep showing up, especially with intensity, they're often pointing to unfinished business from our past—old wounds or patterns still waiting for resolution. By approaching these signals with curiosity instead of judgment, we can start to make sense of them and begin to understand ourselves on a deeper level.

Internal vs. External Validation

Growing up in an environment where your feelings were questioned or dismissed can have long-lasting effects. Over time, this can lead to deep self-doubt, making you question whether your emotions are valid or if you're truly lovable. This insecurity doesn't just fade as you grow older; it often follows you into your relationships and everyday interactions.

This self-doubt plays out in your relationships—whether with friends, family, or romantic partners. You might find yourself constantly explaining your perspective, seeking validation, or needing to be fully understood. But this drive to "get to the root of things" is often less about resolving conflict and more about a deep need to feel seen and validated—a response to years of feeling like your emotions didn't matter.

If left unchecked, this pattern can strain any relationship. Relying on others to affirm your feelings in order to feel emotionally stable creates a cycle of seeking approval without ever feeling truly secure. It reinforces the self-doubt that started in childhood and leads to frustration when others can't provide the constant reassurance you seek.

The key to breaking this cycle is learning how to self-validate. While it's natural to seek understanding from others, true emotional security comes from trusting your own feelings and recognizing that you are the ultimate authority on your emotions. If your sense of worth relies solely on hearing "You're right" from others, your relationships will suffer. Stability comes when you no longer depend on external validation but can confidently validate your own experiences.

Self-Sabotage

Sometimes, we feel like we're making progress, only to take several steps back and feeling like we're back to square one. Despite our efforts, the lack of real progress can be frustrating, leaving us doubting our abilities and questioning our worth. It can feel like we're stuck in place, no matter how hard we work.

Self-sabotage is a defense mechanism we develop to protect ourselves from potential pain, like rejection, failure, or even uncertainty. Unfortunately, it traps us in cycles of behaviors that work against us, preventing us from reaching our full potential. This self-defeating pattern keeps us from achieving what we truly want in life.

Breaking this cycle requires self-awareness, focused effort, and a willingness to replace harmful habits with positive ones. Often, the feeling of being stuck is rooted in limiting beliefs—deeply ingrained thoughts about our capabilities and worth. These beliefs create invisible barriers that stop us from moving forward and cause us to sabotage our own progress.

Common forms of self-sabotage include procrastinating on important tasks, avoiding challenges that push you out of your comfort zone, or making excuses for behaviors that aren't serving you. You might find yourself not expressing your feelings, breaking promises you make to yourself, or pushing yourself to burnout. Staying in unhealthy relationships, avoiding opportunities out of fear, or setting perfectionistic goals can also be part of this cycle.

At the core of self-sabotage are limiting beliefs—thoughts that keep us stuck. The kicker is that we're often unaware of these! Beliefs like "I'm not good enough" create feelings of inadequacy, leading to procrastination or strained relationships. The belief "I don't deserve success" can cause you to undermine your efforts or avoid opportunities out of fear of being seen as a fraud. The idea that "change is too difficult" makes it easy to stay in unhealthy patterns, even when they harm you. Whether it's avoiding help for an addiction or sticking with negative habits, these beliefs are powerful forces that keep us from making meaningful changes.

Linda's Story

Linda, a 47-year-old attorney, had built a respectable career in a well-known law firm, yet she constantly felt stuck in her professional growth. Despite her experience and a strong track record, she found herself unable to secure a partnership or even take on more high-profile cases. Linda often worked long hours, accepted complex assignments, and kept herself informed about changes in the legal field, but her progress seemed to stall just as she approached the next level of success. The lack of recognition and advancement left her doubting her abilities, even though colleagues frequently complimented her work.

Deep down, Linda carried a limiting belief that she wasn't truly deserving of success. Throughout her childhood, she had received mixed messages about her abilities—praised for her hard work but also subtly criticized for not being as naturally gifted as her peers. Over time, Linda internalized a core belief that "I'm not capable of reaching the top," a thought that haunted her as she advanced in her career. Whenever an important opportunity arose—whether it was leading a major case or pushing for partnership—Linda would hesitate, procrastinate, or over-prepare to the point of burnout, ultimately undermining her chances of success. This self-sabotage reinforced her belief that she didn't truly belong at the top.

As Linda continued to grapple with this pattern, she began to notice how it impacted not only her work but also her personal life. She would avoid networking events, stay silent in important meetings, and shy away from asserting her value to her superiors, afraid that if she pushed too hard, she might face rejection. At the same time, she remained in a comfortable yet unfulfilling position, telling herself that "it's better to stay where it's safe" rather than risk failure by stepping into the unknown. This belief kept Linda stuck in a loop of self-doubt and frustration, making her wonder why she couldn't break free despite her efforts. She did all of this without any awareness of the driving force behind it.

Linda's story took a positive turn when a chance conversation with a colleague sparked her curiosity about personal development and limiting beliefs. Linda gradually uncovered the deep-rooted narratives that had shaped her self-doubt. She learned to recognize the subtle ways her childhood experiences had influenced her thinking and, for the first time, saw how her fear of not being "naturally gifted" had been steering her decisions.

With this new self-awareness, Linda started to challenge her inner critic. Instead of over-preparing out of fear, she focused on trusting her expertise and embracing imperfection as part of growth. She practiced speaking up in meetings, sharing her ideas confidently without second-guessing herself. She also made a conscious effort to network, not as a performance but as a genuine exchange of ideas. Slowly but surely, these shifts built her confidence and visibility within the firm.

A year later, Linda applied for partnership—not from a place of desperation to prove herself, but from a genuine belief that she deserved it. This time, her application stood out not just because of her impressive track record but because her leadership presence was undeniable. She secured the partnership, but more importantly, she redefined success on her own terms. Linda's career flourished, not because she changed who she was, but because she finally believed she was enough.

Benign Experiences

Some of the most lasting impacts on our beliefs and self-perception come from experiences that seem benign at first glance. These events, while not overtly traumatic or dramatic, shape how we view ourselves and the world around us. As children, we constantly interpret our surroundings and the behavior of those around us. Even small, seemingly insignificant moments can leave deep impressions. A parent who's too busy to listen to a story, a teacher who praises others but not us, or a peer who leaves us out of a game - these situations may not appear harmful on the surface but can lay the foundation for core beliefs about our worth and place in the world to develop.

What makes these experiences particularly impactful isn't just the event itself, but how we interpret it as children, often with limited understanding. For example, a parent's busy schedule might lead a child to believe their emotions aren't important. Even if the parent didn't mean to harm, the child may internalize the message that they need to suppress their desires or avoid expressing themselves. These beliefs can go unnoticed for years, quietly shaping behavior, relationships, and how we pursue our goals.

As adults, we often revisit these memories without recognizing their deeper meaning. Have you ever thought: "I don't know why I remember that....it seems so stupid." What seems like a small incident from childhood may carry hidden messages about ourselves or others. A memory of being overlooked might create the belief, "I'm not worthy of attention," or "I have to earn love by being perfect." Without realizing it, these interpretations can govern our choices, influence relationships, and shape how we view success and failure.

Reflecting on these experiences and questioning the beliefs we formed as children is a powerful step toward healing. By examining these memories with greater awareness, we can see how our interpretations—rather than the events themselves—created limiting beliefs. This opens the door to rewriting those old stories and embracing a new, healthier narrative about our worth and place in the world.

More Examples

Emily's Story

Take Emily, for example. Growing up, she moved every couple of years due to her father's job, living in six different states and two foreign countries by the time she was 18. This constant change had a profound effect on how she viewed the world. Over time, Emily became acutely aware that nothing stayed the same—friendships, neighborhoods, even the feeling of home were all temporary. As a result, she hesitated to get close to people, worried they'd soon be out of her life like so many before. When she did form connections, they were often intense and fast-paced, as if she was racing against the inevitable separation.

At the same time, Emily developed a strong ability to adapt. She learned to blend into new cultures, pick up on social cues quickly, and navigate new environments with ease. But this constant uprooting left her with a lingering sense that she didn't truly belong anywhere. She felt like a patchwork of different identities, shaped by each place she had lived, but without a solid sense of who she really was. While her experiences made her empathetic and open-minded, they also made her question where "home" really was and whether she could trust that any part of her life would last. This feeling of always being in-between shaped her relationships and her sense of stability, leaving her to wonder if she'd ever find a lasting sense of belonging.

My Own Story

In elementary school, I was elected to run for student council, even though I was a quiet, introverted kid with no interest in student government. The whole idea felt foreign and uncomfortable. Then, as a kind of "punishment," my dad took me to the library and made me write a book report on Mother Teresa. I remember feeling confused and frustrated, not understanding the connection between an election I didn't want and learning about a woman who dedicated her life to service. No one explained the reasoning, so I internalized it as a message that my preferences didn't matter—that my feelings were irrelevant. This memory stuck with me as I grew up.

Years later, I asked my dad why he made me do that. His response caught me off guard—he said it was his way of teaching me about the importance of service. For him, it was about instilling values, but without the explanation, I interpreted it differently. That moment shaped a belief I carried into adulthood: that my desires could be overruled by what others thought was best. It had a lasting impact on how I viewed situations where my voice didn't seem to matter, even though my dad's intentions were very different from how I understood them.

What's Next?

As we dive into Part 1, we'll take a closer look at the experiences that shaped who we are today. Many of the beliefs we hold about ourselves—whether we're aware of them or not—stem from our early relationships and the environment we grew up in. These experiences act as a blueprint for how we navigate the world. Whether it's how we handle conflict, form relationships, or view ourselves, much of it is rooted in how we interpreted things as children. By exploring early influences—whether they come from attachment to caregivers, family dynamics, or traumatic events—we can start to see how they've shaped our adult lives.

The first chapter will delve into attachment theory and family systems to help explain why we behave the way we do now. Many of the struggles we face as adults have deep roots in our childhood experiences. If you grew up with emotionally unavailable parents, family dysfunction, or significant trauma, you might notice those early wounds resurfacing in your adult life. It's not always the big, obvious moments that shape us— often, it's the small, subtle experiences and how we made sense of them as kids.

As you reflect on these early influences, you might start to see familiar patterns in your life, such as trouble trusting others or avoiding conflict. The good news is that by understanding where these patterns come from, you can start to change them. The goal isn't to point fingers or dwell on the past, but to become more aware of how those early experiences continue to affect you—and more importantly, how you can begin to rewrite your story.

This process is about reclaiming control of your narrative. We've all inherited beliefs and habits from our childhood, but we don't have to stay stuck in them. By bringing awareness to these patterns, you can begin to free yourself from self-sabotage and create a life that's more aligned with who you truly are—not the person shaped by the pain or confusion of your past. This chapter marks the first step in that journey.

PART 1

CORE BELIEFS

CHAPTER 1

Impactful Experiences

Everyone sees the world in their own unique way. Two people can go through the exact same situation but come away with completely different interpretations. This is because our core beliefs—those deeply ingrained ideas we hold about ourselves and the world—shape how we make sense of our experiences.

These deeply ingrained perceptions we form early in life affect every area of our existence. From handling conflict to trusting others, these beliefs act as filters through which we interpret the world. The challenge is that many of these beliefs were formed in childhood, when we had limited understanding and control. As adults, we carry these outdated beliefs into new situations, often unaware that they no longer serve us and may be actively holding us back from growth, happiness, and connection.

No one had a perfect childhood; we all carry certain beliefs that no longer serve us and, in some cases, may even be holding us back. But that doesn't mean we're stuck with them forever. While our past shapes our beliefs, we have the power to change them with the right approach.

By exploring our family of origin—the environment and relationships we grew up in—along with other impactful childhood experiences, we can better understand what worked and what didn't. Often, the "wounds" from our early years show up in unexpected ways in adulthood, influencing everything from work challenges to personal relationships. The good news? Once we become aware of these influences, we can rewire our thinking and behavior, making significant improvements in our self-worth and overall well-being.

It doesn't matter if you've been in therapy for years or prefer to tackle things on your own, and it doesn't matter whether your childhood seemed idyllic or deeply challenging. Everyone has the potential to create significant change and address unresolved issues from the past. Through guided self-reflection, real-life examples and practical tools, you can break away from old belief systems and reinvent the way you live.

The true version of you isn't defined by the conditioned thoughts, reactions, or habits you have today. You aren't broken or unworthy; you've simply adopted these beliefs through your past experiences.

The 80/20 Rule

Let's talk about the 80/20 rule for emotional responses. When you react to something, only about 20% of your reaction is actually about what's happening in the moment. The other 80%? That's the ghosts of your past sneaking in—old wounds, patterns, and baggage you might not even realize you're still carrying.

Think about it. You get stung by criticism from a colleague, and suddenly it feels like you're 10 years old again, getting grilled by a parent who made you feel like you weren't good enough. Your reaction might feel huge, but what's really happening is that you're pulling from past experiences without even knowing it. Once you realize this, it's a game changer.

Understanding the 80/20 rule can be a total eye-opener. It makes you pause and think, "Wait a second, am I really this upset about *this*? Or is something else going on here?" It's not that the current situation isn't important—it's just that your brain has a funny way of throwing in unresolved emotional baggage for good measure. That's why your reactions sometimes feel way more intense than the situation calls for.

Knowing this can seriously fast-track your personal growth. When you get that most of your emotional reactions are being fueled by prior impactful experiences, you can start digging into those old issues. Instead of just reacting on autopilot, you can hit pause, get curious, and respond in a way that actually serves you—rather than sabotaging you.

Same Situation, Different Outcomes

Picture two people sitting in the backseat of a car. The driver loses control and crashes head-on into a tree. Both backseat passengers experience the same crash, but their reactions, both immediately and in the long run, could be completely different. Passenger A might check to make sure everyone's okay, take a deep breath, and eventually feel relieved that it's over. But Passenger B might feel shaken, unable to calm down, and carry that fear for months, dreading every car ride. This shows that trauma isn't about the event itself—it's about how the event impacts you. And trauma doesn't always come from big events; it can also come from things that didn't happen, like not getting the emotional care you needed growing up.

A traumatic event triggers an instant reaction in our nervous system, controlling how our body responds to stress. Take the car crash, for example: both passengers likely felt a surge of fear and braced for impact. But once the danger passed, Passenger A might have calmed down and felt safe again. Passenger B, however, could have gotten stuck in that fear, especially if something made the situation worse—like being trapped in the car. If, on top of that, Passenger B was accused of overreacting or their experience was minimized by others, their nervous system might stay stuck in that heightened, defensive state, making recovery even harder.

This shows that people don't always respond to the same experience in the same way. Just like Passenger A and Passenger B, one person might bounce back quickly, while another might struggle to feel safe again. The difference isn't about the event itself but how each person's nervous system handles it, and whether they feel supported afterward. Trauma lingers not just because of what happened, but because of how it affects us emotionally and physically—sometimes long after the moment has passed.

Relational Trauma

Relational trauma isn't always about what happened to us; it's often about what didn't. Feeling ignored or dismissed can be just as damaging as outright abuse. These experiences teach our bodies to view the lack of care as a threat, making us hyper-aware of how others treat us. That's why triggers show up in daily interactions, especially with the people closest to us. We end up reacting defensively or anxiously, even when there's no real danger. This makes it tough to form healthy relationships because we're constantly dealing with the effects of what we missed out on in those early connections.

One of my favorite quotes comes from Gabor Maté: *"Trauma is not what happens to you. It's what happens inside you, as a result of what happened to you."* It's a powerful reminder that it's not just about the external events themselves—it's about the lasting emotional and psychological wounds they leave behind. It changes how you see yourself, how you relate to others, and how you view the world. For example, having an emotionally absent parent might leave you feeling unworthy, making it hard to trust others long after those early experiences. Healing isn't just about moving past the event itself; it's about working through those internal scars and learning to nurture yourself.

Now, unless you've been living under a rock, you've probably heard the word "trauma" getting tossed around everywhere lately. It's a term that's become pretty mainstream, but what does it actually mean? Trauma can mess with your emotions, your thoughts, and even your physical health. When we think of *"trauma,"* most of us picture the big stuff—what we call *"Big T trauma."* You know, the really life-shattering events like sexual assault, surviving a war, or living through a natural disaster. This kind of trauma is usually tied to PTSD, where people experience flashbacks, intense anxiety, and all kinds of overwhelming symptoms. PTSD tends to be more fear-based, with the trauma rooted in a specific, terrifying event.

But there's another kind of trauma that flies under the radar, *"little t trauma,"* which refers to personal events that are distressing but not life threatening. This can include relational trauma, or attachment trauma, also known as complex trauma (C-PTSD). While *Big T* trauma is dramatic and easy to spot, *little t* trauma is sneaky and often overlooked. It's made up of those ongoing stressors that quietly pile up over time—emotional abuse, neglect, chronic illness, or even the loss of a significant relationship. The problem with *little t* trauma is that it doesn't fit the stereotypical image of trauma, so people often don't realize they're carrying it. With C-PTSD, the trauma is so woven into everyday life that it stops feeling like trauma at all—it's just life as you know it.

Little t trauma can be just as harmful, if not more, because it hides in plain sight. People might feel confused or ashamed, thinking their struggles don't count because they haven't survived a "big" traumatic event. But the impact on their mental health is real, leading to feelings of worthlessness, chronic anxiety, depression, and emotional instability. Unlike PTSD, which is linked to one major event, C-PTSD builds up over years of distress, making it more complex to deal with. It's characterized by a vicious inner critic, toxic shame, social anxiety, emotional flashbacks, and self-abandonment. Generally, C-PTSD is more rooted in shame, whereas PTSD is more rooted in fear.

Understanding the difference between *Big T* and *little t* trauma helps validate the full range of human suffering. It ensures that no one's trauma is dismissed, and that everyone gets the empathy and support they deserve. By acknowledging both, we can build a more compassionate approach to mental health and create better systems of care and healing.

Family Systems

Generational trauma is the emotional and psychological pain that gets passed down from one generation to the next, like an invisible family heirloom no one asked for. It can quietly shape family dynamics and individual behaviors, often without anyone realizing the full extent of its impact. Understanding how this trauma is handed down is crucial for breaking the cycle and finally finding healing.

One way this trauma gets passed down is through learned behaviors and coping mechanisms. Kids absorb how their parents deal with stress and adversity, sometimes even mimicking those unhealthy patterns. If parents haven't processed their own trauma, their reactions can create an atmosphere of instability and fear, which the child picks up on and carries forward into adulthood. These patterns can get so deeply ingrained that they stick around, even when the original traumatic patterns are ancient history.

But it doesn't stop there—trauma can also be passed down biologically. Research in epigenetics shows that severe trauma can change a person's genes, altering how their body handles stress. These genetic changes can be passed to their children, making them more prone to anxiety, depression, and other mental health issues. So, it's not just behaviors being handed down—it's literally in the DNA.

Another powerful way trauma is passed down? In utero. When a pregnant person experiences high levels of stress or trauma, those stress hormones, like cortisol, can cross the placenta and impact the developing baby. This exposure can increase the child's risk for anxiety, depression, and other stress-related issues later in life. That means trauma can leave its mark even before a person is born.

The cycle of generational trauma continues until someone decides to break it. And let's be honest—it's hard work. It takes therapy, self-reflection, and a willingness to confront painful family histories. But by recognizing the trauma and how it's impacted family dynamics, individuals can begin to develop healthier ways of coping and interacting. The payoff? Breaking the cycle for future generations.

Healing generational trauma isn't just about you—it's about creating a healthier future for your family, too. While the legacy of trauma can be long and deep, the potential for healing is just as powerful. And that healing can ripple through generations, offering hope and resilience for years to come.

Olena's Story

Olena, a 40-year-old successful financial analyst, lived with the core belief that she always had to be prepared for the worst and could not fully trust others. Known for her meticulous planning and ability to foresee potential problems, she struggled to delegate tasks at work, fearing others wouldn't meet her standards. This constant need for control and preparedness led to long hours, burnout, and significant stress as she felt solely responsible for the outcomes of her projects.

In her personal life, Olena found it challenging to form deep, trusting relationships. She kept people at a distance, wary of being let down or hurt. This affected her friendships and romantic relationships, as she found it hard to open up and be vulnerable. Her partners often perceived her as emotionally distant and overly cautious, creating tension and misunderstandings.

The root of Olena's core belief lay in her family's history of displacement and loss. Her grandparents, who were refugees fleeing the Soviet repression and the violent upheavals of World War II, endured severe hardship and trauma, losing homes, family members, and their sense of security. These experiences left a lasting impact on Olena's parents, who were born in exile and grew up in an environment of scarcity and fear.

Olena grew up surrounded by stories of her grandparents' and parents' struggles. Her grandparents often spoke about their harrowing escape to safety, the loss of loved ones, and the difficulties of rebuilding their lives in a new land. Olena's parents, having grown up in a constant state of uncertainty, emphasized the importance of hard work, self-reliance, and always being prepared for the worst. They were always cautious, expressing fear and mistrust of others, which they passed on to Olena.

From these generational experiences, Olena developed her core belief that she had to always be prepared for the worst and could not fully trust others. This belief was reinforced by her family's emphasis on self-sufficiency and their frequent discussions about the dangers and uncertainties of the world. Olena internalized the idea that she needed to be constantly vigilant and that relying on others could lead to disappointment or betrayal.

The generational trauma Olena carried manifested in her daily life as chronic anxiety and a pervasive sense of mistrust. Her grandparents' and parents' experiences with displacement and loss had left an indelible mark on her subconscious, shaping her core beliefs and behavior patterns. Although she did not endure the original traumas, their legacy continued to influence her interactions and view of the world.

Olena's story highlights how transgenerational trauma can be passed down through narratives, behaviors, and deeply ingrained beliefs, affecting individuals even if they hadn't directly experienced the traumatic events.

Olena's story began to shift when she started uncovering how her core belief—that she always had to be prepared for the worst and could not fully trust others—was rooted in her family's history of displacement and loss. Through therapy, she recognized how the generational trauma passed down from her grandparents and parents had shaped her chronic anxiety, need for control, and difficulty forming deep connections. With this awareness, Olena gradually learned to challenge her mistrust, set healthier boundaries around work, and open up emotionally in her relationships. As she practiced vulnerability and allowed herself to rely on others, she experienced a profound sense of relief and connection, realizing that true security came not from constant vigilance but from meaningful, trusting relationships.

Emotionally Immature Parents

Having a critical or emotionally absent parent can deeply affect how you see yourself, others, and the world. When a parent is constantly critical, it's easy to grow up feeling like you're never quite enough. Instead of feeling valued, you may internalize their criticism, believing there's something inherently wrong with you—that you're flawed or unworthy of love. This creates a core belief that you have to be perfect just to earn a sliver of approval, and let's be honest, that's an exhausting way to live.

On the flip side, if your parent is emotionally absent—there physically, but nowhere to be found emotionally—you're left feeling neglected, like you don't matter. Without that emotional connection or validation, you might start to believe your needs and feelings aren't important. This can lead to a deep-seated belief that you're unlovable or undeserving of attention, which makes forming healthy, trusting relationships down the road a real challenge.

Your early experiences don't just shape how you see yourself—they influence how you view others and the world around you. If you had a critical parent, you might expect judgment and harshness from others, leading to defensiveness and a constant need to prove yourself, often resulting in anxiety and a fear of failure. On the other hand, an emotionally absent parent may have taught you to see people as unreliable, making trust difficult and deep connections even harder. This can leave you feeling isolated, viewing the world as indifferent and believing you must navigate it alone.

Emotionally immature parents have a way of putting their own feelings and needs above those of their kids. This typically results from that being the dynamic in which they grew up (remember that generational trauma we learned about). When children express emotions, they're often met with negative reactions, discouraging them from opening up. These parents rarely take accountability for their actions, shifting blame onto others and struggling to regulate their emotions, leading to unpredictable behavior. They also fail to respect boundaries, undermining their children's sense of self and safety. Their lack of self-reflection keeps the cycle of emotional neglect and misunderstanding spinning, generation after generation.

Your parents may have provided over and above what you needed on the surface—new clothes, the latest gadgets, the best education—but were still emotionally absent. This kind of disconnect can leave you believing that your feelings don't matter. Picture this: you grow up in a home where you're given everything—a brand new car, fancy vacations—but your parents are always too busy with work or other obligations to care about your emotional world. When you try to talk about your struggles at school or issues with friends, you're made to feel ungrateful, like asking for emotional support is selfish when you already have so much. Over time, you start to push down your emotions, convinced that as long as your physical needs are met, your feelings aren't important. As an adult, this pattern sticks with you. You tell yourself things like, "I have no reason to complain," or "Other people have it worse." That guilt keeps you from acknowledging your emotional needs, leaving you disconnected from your own inner world.

According to Dr. Lindsay Gibson (2015), different types of emotionally immature parents affect their children in various ways. *Emotional parents* are driven by their feelings, overreacting to small issues and seeking comfort through others or substances. They're unpredictable, swinging from being overly involved to abruptly withdrawing. *Driven parents* may seem like they have it all together, highly invested in their children's lives, but underneath, they're controlling and lack true empathy, pushing their kids to adopt their own goals and values. *Passive parents* avoid conflict at all costs. While they may seem emotionally available, they fail to provide guidance and often allow abuse or neglect by deferring to a more dominant partner. Then there are *rejecting parents*, who prefer to be left alone, ruling the household with outbursts, isolation, or strict commands. Affection and engagement are minimal, leaving the entire family walking on eggshells to avoid setting them off.

Understanding these dynamics is key to recognizing the impact emotionally immature parents have. It's not about blaming them, but about gaining the self-awareness needed to liberate yourself and create emotional independence.

John's Story

John, a 36-year-old successful IT specialist, built a reputation for his strong work ethic and perfectionistic tendencies. However, beneath his professional success lay a deep-seated core belief that he wasn't good enough and needed to continuously prove his worth through productivity and achievement. This belief drove him to take on more work than he could handle, working long hours, often skipping breaks, and feeling that any misstep or failure would confirm his internal sense of incompetence. The constant pressure resulted in burnout, stress, and a persistent sense of dissatisfaction.

In his personal life, John found it difficult to connect emotionally with others. His romantic relationships suffered, as partners perceived him as emotionally distant and detached, making it hard for him to form deep, meaningful connections. His friends also noticed that he seemed absent during conversations, preoccupied with the need to stay busy or distracted.

In an effort to manage his feelings of inadequacy and relentless pressure to succeed, John increasingly turned to self-medicating behaviors that masked his emotional distress. After long, exhausting workdays, he often numbed himself with several drinks, convincing himself it was just a way to "unwind," though it frequently led to restless nights and groggy mornings. On weekends, he binged on junk food while mindlessly scrolling through social media or gaming for hours, using the constant stimulation to drown out the nagging sense of emptiness and failure lurking beneath the surface. What started as occasional coping mechanisms gradually became habitual, leaving John caught in a cycle where temporary relief only deepened his disconnection from his emotions and the people around him.

The root of John's core belief lay in his upbringing. He grew up in a household where his parents were emotionally unavailable, often preoccupied with their own struggles. His father, a workaholic, frequently emphasized the importance of hard work and achievement as measures of success, while his mother, overwhelmed with her own emotional burdens, wasn't able to provide consistent validation or emotional support. As a result, John learned early on that his value came from what he could accomplish, rather than who he was as a person.

This lack of emotional support left John feeling unworthy and unseen. To cope, he adopted the belief that he needed to constantly prove himself through achievement, productivity, and busyness. He developed a habit of avoiding his feelings of inadequacy and loneliness by staying busy—whether at work or by distracting himself with food, alcohol, or technology. Each time John reached for these distractions, he reinforced the core belief that he wasn't enough and that avoiding his feelings was easier than confronting them.

John's story highlights how negative core beliefs, tied to early life experiences, can lead to self-sabotaging behaviors like numbing through distractions. By turning to quick fixes like food, alcohol, or screen time, he avoided dealing with his emotions and reinforced his underlying belief of inadequacy. The cycle of avoidance left him disconnected from his true self and from others, perpetuating feelings of loneliness and dissatisfaction.

Through our work together, John began to explore the connection between his core belief and his behavior patterns. He learned that his worth was not tied to his productivity and that avoiding his uncomfortable feelings only magnified them over time. By addressing the root cause of his belief and learning to sit with discomfort rather than numb it, John began to break the cycle of avoidance and worked toward living more authentically.

Early Thoughts, Lasting Impact

The way we understand the world as children plays a huge role in shaping the beliefs we carry into adulthood. As kids, we don't have all the information or emotional maturity needed to make sense of what's happening around us, so we end up filling in the blanks on our own. This often leads to thought patterns like cognitive distortions, egocentrism, and magical thinking—patterns that create powerful core beliefs about ourselves and our place in the world. The kicker? These beliefs tend to stick with us, often fueling feelings of guilt, shame, or the sense that we're not good enough.

Cognitive distortions occur when kids misinterpret situations because they lack the full picture. When faced with something confusing or upsetting, they come up with their own stories to explain it. For example, if a parent becomes distant or suddenly absent, a child might believe they did something wrong to cause it. These misinterpretations can plant the seeds of lifelong beliefs like "I'm unlovable" or "Everything is my fault," which can continue to shape self-worth and relationships well into adulthood.

Egocentrism in children adds another layer to this confusion. At this developmental stage, kids naturally see themselves as the center of everything. If their parents are fighting or there's a major life change, they might assume it's somehow their fault, even when it has nothing to do with them. This can create a belief that they're responsible for other people's problems or happiness, a burden that many carry into adulthood, often leading to feelings of inadequacy or self-blame.

Magical thinking takes this idea even further. It's the belief that their thoughts or actions have the power to control the outside world. A child might think, "If I had been better behaved, my dad wouldn't have gotten sick" or "If I hadn't done that bad thing, my parents wouldn't have gotten divorced." This type of thinking can create harmful beliefs like "I let people down" or "I cause bad things to happen," leading to deep-seated guilt and shame that stick around long after childhood. Over time, these early misunderstandings become core beliefs that silently shape how we see ourselves and the world, often without us even realizing it.

Discovery Prompt:
Life Event & Memory Timeline

Spend 10-15 minutes creating a timeline of significant moments and memories from your life. These could be major events or small, seemingly insignificant memories that stand out to you. For each, note:

1. **The year or age** the event or memory occurred.

2. **What happened** (e.g., a major milestone, a small conversation, or a simple moment).

3. **Why it stands out** - whether it was a turning point or just something that stuck with you over time.

Focus on both the big and small moments that have influenced your personal growth or stuck with you for any reason, even if they seem benign.

CHAPTER 2

Ages & Stages: How Core Beliefs are Developed

To truly understand how core beliefs are formed, we need to take a journey back to the earliest years of our lives. These foundational stages—from infancy through adolescence—are where the deep-seated beliefs about ourselves and the world began to take root. The interactions we had with our caregivers, alongside significant life events, set the stage for our future emotional and psychological well-being.

Erik Erikson's Psychosocial Development Theory (1963) outlines key stages of development that help highlight the critical conflicts and growth opportunities we faced as we matured. Each stage presents unique challenges and milestones that contribute to the formation of core beliefs and our overall self-perception. From learning to trust others in our earliest years to solidifying a sense of identity during adolescence, these stages are pivotal in shaping the way we view ourselves and our place in the world. Francine Shapiro (1987) took this one step further and identified core belief clusters related to these developmental plateaus, which we'll explore more in Part 2.

In this chapter, I'll break down these crucial stages of development and explore how early experiences can lead to either positive or negative core beliefs. Using real-life examples and relatable stories, I'll show how these beliefs manifest in adulthood, shaping your behaviors, relationships, and overall self-perception. By understanding these developmental stages, you'll gain valuable insight into the origins of your core beliefs and open the door to greater self-awareness.

I invite you to trace your own path from infancy to adolescence, reflecting on key developmental milestones and the lasting influence they've had on your life. This exploration will provide the foundation for understanding how your early years continue to impact your present, and more importantly, how you can begin to address and transform the beliefs that no longer serve you.

Ages 0-2: Survival & Existence (preverbal)

The first couple of years of life, from birth to age two, are all about survival. During this time, we rely entirely on our caregivers to meet basic needs like food, safety, and comfort. How consistently these needs are met builds the foundation of trust and security that shape our worldview. This is where Erik Erikson's concept of "trust versus mistrust" comes into play. When caregivers are loving and attentive, we learn to trust the world around us. But if those needs aren't met reliably, the world can start to feel unpredictable and unsafe.

As we navigate this phase, we're also beginning to develop a sense of self-worth. Even at such a young age, the way caregivers respond to our needs shapes how we see ourselves. When our cries for food, comfort, or affection are met with love and care, we start to feel valued. This sense of being important and cherished just as we are becomes the foundation for healthy self-esteem as we grow.

During these early years, we also start to understand emotional authenticity—figuring out how, when, and with whom we can express our feelings. If a caregiver consistently offers comfort when we are distressed, we learn it's safe to be open about our emotions. On the flip side, if our caregiver's response is neglectful or inconsistent, we may begin to hold back, unsure of when it's safe to show our true feelings.

What's particularly fascinating is that these experiences happen before we have the words to describe them—they're preverbal. We don't recall memories from this stage like we do later in life, but the experiences are deeply embedded in our bodies and subconscious minds. These early interactions influence how we respond to stress, form attachments, and feel secure, even if we're not aware of it. When our needs aren't adequately met, it can lead to negative core beliefs, such as feeling unworthy or mistrustful, or believing our needs don't matter. This stage of life isn't just about physical survival; it's about the emotional and psychological nurturing that helps us grow into a healthy, authentic individual.

Emma's Story

Emma, a 28-year-old graphic designer at a creative agency, often felt overwhelmed by the nagging belief that she was abandoned and alone. Despite her impressive artistic talent and recognition in her field, Emma constantly battled a deep sense of isolation and feared that those close to her would eventually leave her.

In her personal life, Emma struggled to form and maintain close relationships. Trusting others didn't come easy for her, and she often anticipated rejection, causing her to withdraw emotionally. In romantic relationships, Emma's fear of abandonment led her to become overly clingy, constantly seeking reassurance. This behavior often pushed her partners away. Even her friendships suffered because she found it hard to believe that anyone genuinely cared for her, often interpreting benign actions as signs of impending abandonment.

This deeply ingrained belief that she was alone and unlovable dated back to Emma's early childhood. Her mother suffered from severe postpartum depression after Emma was born, which severely impacted her ability to bond with her daughter. During Emma's infancy, her mother was often emotionally unavailable, distant, and unable to respond consistently to Emma's needs. As a result, Emma never developed the secure attachment necessary for a healthy emotional foundation.

Emma's father, who was preoccupied with work and managing the household, couldn't fill the emotional void left by her mother. He often left Emma in the care of relatives or babysitters, further contributing to her feelings of abandonment. As Emma grew older, these early experiences manifested in a pervasive belief that she was unlovable and destined to be alone.

During her school years, Emma was a quiet and withdrawn child, finding solace in art and creativity. She excelled in her studies and developed a keen eye for design, but her social interactions were limited. Emma's teachers and peers often described her as shy and reserved, unaware of the deep-seated fear of abandonment driving her behavior. Her successes in school and later in her career provided temporary boosts to her self-esteem, but the underlying belief that she was abandoned and alone persisted.

Emma's journey toward healing began when a painful breakup with a partner who grew frustrated by her constant need for reassurance forced her to confront the patterns in her relationships. She had spent most of the relationship anxiously analyzing his every word and action, convinced that at any moment, he would leave her. When he needed space, she panicked, sending multiple texts or showing up unannounced, desperate for validation. Over time, he became emotionally withdrawn, telling her he felt suffocated and unable to meet her endless need for reassurance. When he finally ended things, Emma was devastated but also forced to acknowledge a painful truth—her fear of abandonment had become a self-fulfilling prophecy.

Seeking therapy in her late-twenties, she began to uncover the origins of her core belief and understand how her mother's postpartum depression had impacted her emotional development. I introduced her to attachment theory and helped Emma recognize how her fear of abandonment and anxious attachment style had shaped her behaviors.

With time and effort, Emma started to challenge her negative beliefs, practicing self-compassion and learning to communicate her needs more effectively. Emma also began opening up to her friends about her struggles, surprised by the warmth and support she received—proof that she wasn't as alone as she had always feared. As she rebuilt her self-esteem and formed more secure attachments, Emma realized that while the fear of abandonment might still surface, it no longer controlled her life.

Ages 2-4: Control

Between the ages of 2 and 4, we enter a crucial phase of exploring control and independence. This is the period where we start asserting ourselves, making decisions, and testing limits. Erik Erikson refers to this as the stage of "autonomy versus shame and doubt." When caregivers support our need to explore and make independent choices, while still offering guidance, we develop a healthy sense of autonomy. But when caregivers are overly critical or controlling, we may start to feel ashamed or doubtful about our abilities.

During this time, we begin to understand what we can and can't control. We start taking on appropriate responsibilities and learning when it's okay to let go. This could look like insisting on dressing ourselves, choosing what to eat for breakfast, or deciding when to use the potty. These small acts of independence are actually big milestones in our journey to learning decision-making and taking responsibility. It's important for caregivers to create an environment where we can make safe choices within boundaries, helping us understand the limits of our control without feeling overwhelmed.

As we move through this stage, we also start to grasp the bigger picture of control and responsibility. We realize that while we can choose what toy to play with, some things are simply out of our hands. This understanding builds resilience and adaptability—skills we'll rely on throughout life. Caregivers who encourage these little steps towards independence help us feel secure and confident in our growing abilities.

On the flip side, if we don't get the opportunity to explore autonomy, or if our attempts at control are constantly shut down, we might develop negative beliefs about ourselves. We may feel powerless, incapable of making good decisions, or become overly reliant on others for approval and guidance. This stage isn't just about gaining control—it's about learning how to balance independence with responsibility, setting the stage for a confident, capable person later in life.

I'm in the thick of it with this stage right now. Every morning with my 4-year-old feels like stepping into a high-stakes negotiation. I suggest pants; he counters with a superhero cape and mismatched socks. By the time we settle on something halfway reasonable, it feels like I've just brokered a peace deal—next up, the battle over brushing his teeth.

Raj's Story

Raj, a 35-year-old financial analyst at a leading investment firm, came to me seeking help because he felt overwhelmed by his constant need for control and inflexibility. Despite his successful career and reputation for precision, these things had started to take a toll on his personal life. Raj meticulously planned his daily schedule, from the time he woke up to every detail of his work and home life. Any deviation from his plan caused him significant stress, leading to anxiety and frustration. In his relationships, Raj's need for control often created tension. He tended to make decisions on behalf of his partner, from weekend plans to more significant life choices, which left his partner feeling stifled.

The roots of Raj's need for control were traced back to his childhood, during which his mother, wanting to ensure everything was perfect, did things like insisting on picking out his clothes and dressing him each day. She made sure he always looked presentable and followed a strict routine, leaving little room for Raj to make any decisions on his own. While her intentions were protective and well-meaning, Raj began to internalize the idea that things needed to be done a certain way to avoid judgment or disapproval. Over time, this developed into a belief that if he wasn't in control of the details, things might go wrong.

As Raj grew older, these patterns of control reinforced themselves. In school, Raj thrived in structured environments, excelling academically and maintaining a tight schedule to ensure success. His teachers praised him for his diligence, but underneath, Raj felt constant pressure to maintain control over every aspect of his life. He avoided group projects where he couldn't take the lead and focused on solo tasks where he was responsible for the outcome.

Entering the fast-paced world of finance only solidified this mindset. In a field where precision and risk management are essential, Raj's need for control aligned perfectly with his career. But with high stakes also came intense stress. Any unexpected issue at work—whether a last-minute client request or a fluctuating market—could trigger deep anxiety for Raj, reinforcing his belief that he must always be in control to avoid mistakes or failure.

It wasn't until Raj began experiencing recurrent physical symptoms of stress, such as tension headaches and difficulty sleeping, that he sought me out for therapy. He admitted that his need for control was no longer serving him; it was beginning to harm both his personal well-being and his relationships. Together, we began exploring the origins of this belief, starting with his early experiences of his mother's overinvolvement in managing the details of his life. Raj started to realize that his need to control everything wasn't just about work or relationships—it was a lifelong pattern rooted in his childhood experiences and reinforced by subsequent ones.

In therapy, Raj learned techniques to manage his anxiety around control. We worked on mindfulness exercises and gradual exposure to situations in which he could loosen his grip on control, such as delegating tasks at work or letting his partner plan a weekend without his input. It wasn't easy for Raj at first, but over time, he saw that letting go of control didn't lead to the worst case scenarios he feared. He has continued to work on accepting that not everything can be controlled, and that it's okay to trust others and be open to change.

Ages 3-5: Responsibility

Between the ages of 3 and 5, we begin to get a clearer sense of responsibility and independence. This is when we start to realize we have certain duties, but we also learn that we're not responsible for everything—especially other people's feelings. Erik Erikson refers to this phase as the "initiative versus guilt" stage. When caregivers support our efforts to take on new tasks and responsibilities, we develop a healthy sense of initiative. But if caregivers are overly critical or controlling, we may start to feel guilty or overly responsible for things that are beyond our control.

At this age, we often start exploring our independence more actively. We might help with small tasks like setting the table, dressing ourselves, or trying to care for a pet. These experiences teach us the value of responsibility and help build our confidence. It's important for caregivers to let us attempt these tasks and offer support, even when mistakes happen.

This way, we learn that it's okay to make errors and that trying again is part of the process.

A crucial lesson during this stage is understanding that while we can control our own actions, we are not responsible for other people's emotions. For example, we might feel guilty if we see a parent upset or a friend crying, assuming it's our fault. Caregivers need to teach us that everyone is responsible for managing their own feelings, and it's not our job to fix or carry others' emotional burdens. This helps us develop healthy emotional boundaries and protects us from taking on too much responsibility for others.

If we don't receive the right guidance during this stage, we may develop harmful beliefs about responsibility. We might start to feel like everything is our fault, leading to excessive guilt or anxiety. Alternatively, we could grow up believing we have to take care of others at the expense of our own needs. By teaching us to balance responsibility and understand our limits, caregivers help us build the foundation for becoming confident, emotionally healthy individuals.

Ananya's Story

Ananya, a 45-year-old operations manager, felt overwhelmed by the constant pressure to be responsible for everyone around her. Although she was successful at work and adept at managing multiple projects, this belief was causing her significant stress. At work, Ananya often overstepped her responsibilities, taking on extra tasks to cover for colleagues, while in her personal life, she struggled to set boundaries and frequently overextended herself to care for family and friends, even at the expense of her own well-being.

Ananya's overwhelming sense of responsibility was deeply rooted in her early childhood, where she was not just the oldest child but often treated as a second parent. Her parents, both working long hours to make ends meet, relied heavily on her to care for her younger siblings—managing their routines, helping with homework, and even mediating conflicts. Moments of her own frustration or exhaustion were dismissed with reminders of how "mature" and "reliable" she was, leaving little space for her to express vulnerability.

This dynamic was further reinforced when, at just 12 years old, she stepped in to manage the household during her mother's brief illness, an experience that solidified her belief that others' well-being depended entirely on her. Over time, these patterns became ingrained, shaping not only her sense of self-worth but also her understanding of what it meant to be "good enough"—a belief that quietly followed her into adulthood, creating the very burnout she struggled to escape.

As an adult, Ananya's belief that she needed to hold everything together created tension in both her professional and personal life. At work, she frequently volunteered for tasks that weren't her responsibility, and her colleagues came to depend on her. In her personal life, she often played the role of caregiver, struggling to say no and sacrificing her own needs to support others. Compounding this was her hyper-independence—avoiding delegation or asking for help because she didn't trust others to do things the "right" way. This left her exhausted and burnt out.

We explored the origins of Ananya's belief, tracing it back to her childhood experiences and the praise she received for being dependable. By understanding how these early experiences shaped her, Ananya began to challenge this belief and practice setting boundaries. She learned to say no without guilt, accept help from others, and let go of the need to control every situation. Over time, she tested these new behaviors, realizing that the world didn't fall apart when she stepped back or allowed others to take responsibility.

Ages 3-6: Worthiness

Between the ages of 3 and 6, we begin to develop a sense of worthiness. This is a critical time when we need to feel that we are lovable and valuable just as we are. We need to know that we matter, our needs can be met, and that there are people we can rely on for support. It's about learning to accept ourselves fully and understanding that we can thrive no matter what life throws our way.

This ties into Erik Erikson's "initiative versus guilt" stage. At this point, we start to take initiative and explore new things, looking to our caregivers for reassurance and validation. When caregivers provide love, encouragement, and support, we develop confidence and a strong sense of self-worth. But if caregivers are overly critical or dismissive, we may start to feel guilty, believing that we're not good enough. Positive reinforcement is key here to help us build a solid foundation of worthiness and self-esteem.

During this period, we also begin to understand and accept our own needs. We start figuring out how to express those needs and who we can count on for help. Caregivers play a massive role in this by being responsive and showing us that our needs matter. This responsiveness teaches us that it's okay to ask for help and that we are deserving of care and attention. As a result, we develop a healthy sense of self-worth and learn how to advocate for ourselves as we grow.

If we don't get the love and support we need during this stage, we can develop negative beliefs about ourselves, such as feeling unlovable, worthless, or like we don't matter. These feelings can follow us into adulthood, impacting our self-esteem and relationships. Ensuring we know we are loved and valued, no matter what, helps build a strong sense of worthiness that will carry us through future challenges with resilience and confidence.

David's Story

David, a 48-year-old civil engineer at a construction firm, often felt overwhelmed by the nagging belief that he was unlovable and unworthy. Despite being professionally competent and respected by his colleagues, he constantly battled feelings of inadequacy and worthlessness. These beliefs impacted his self-esteem, creating a deep sense of insecurity that pervaded both his personal and professional life.

In his personal life, David's belief that he was unlovable manifested in several ways. He struggled to form and maintain close relationships, feeling that he didn't deserve love or attention. In romantic relationships, David became overly accommodating, constantly seeking validation from his partner to prove his worth. This need for reassurance led him to prioritize his partner's needs over his own, which created imbalance and often pushed his partners away, reinforcing his fears of being unworthy of love. Even in his friendships, David found it difficult to believe that others genuinely valued him, often interpreting benign actions as signs that he was unimportant or easily forgotten.

The origin of David's belief that he was unlovable and unworthy could be traced back to his emotionally distant childhood.

Growing up, David's parents were often preoccupied—his father consumed by work and his mother struggling with undiagnosed depression—which left little room for emotional connection. He vividly remembers coming home excited to show his parents a drawing he'd made in second grade, only to receive a distracted nod before they shifted their focus back to their own concerns. Moments like these, small but cumulative, left David feeling invisible, as if his emotions and achievements didn't matter. Over time, he internalized the belief that he had to earn love through perfection and constant accommodation, shaping the patterns of self-doubt and insecurity that followed him into adulthood.

As David entered adolescence, these feelings of unworthiness intensified. Despite excelling academically and in sports, he struggled to feel that his successes mattered. Praise from teachers and peers felt shallow, and David often dismissed compliments, convinced that he was just pretending to be someone worthy of admiration. Deep down, he believed that if people truly knew him, they would see that he wasn't deserving of love or attention.

This pattern carried into David's professional life. His job as a civil engineer was demanding, requiring precision and problem-solving skills. Though he was good at his work, any minor mistake or setback would trigger a wave of self-doubt, causing David to feel inadequate. He constantly felt the need to prove himself, yet no amount of success could quiet the internal voice that told him he wasn't good enough. These feelings of unworthiness created immense pressure, which further reinforced his belief that he was not worthy of respect or recognition.

Eventually, the weight of these beliefs became too much for David to bear. He sought me out for therapy when he realized that these patterns were affecting his relationships, career, and overall happiness. We began exploring the roots of his belief that he was unlovable and unworthy, tracing it back to those early childhood experiences when he felt emotionally neglected and overlooked. We discussed how his parents' lack of emotional engagement, though unintentional, had shaped his core belief that he didn't matter.

As David started to understand where these beliefs came from, we worked on strategies to help him build a healthier sense of self-worth. We challenged the negative thoughts that constantly reinforced his feelings of inadequacy, and David practiced self-compassion, learning to treat himself with the kindness he often extended to others. Over time, he began to test these new beliefs, allowing himself to accept compliments and acknowledge his accomplishments without immediately dismissing them.

David's progress was gradual, but he began to notice changes. In his personal life, he started communicating more openly in his relationships, sharing his fears and needs with his partner and friends. This openness led to deeper, more meaningful connections, and David slowly started to believe that he was indeed valued by the people in his life. At work, he became more comfortable accepting praise and took pride in his achievements without feeling like an imposter.

Ages 4-7: Competency

Between the ages of 4 and 7, we reach a stage where we begin to develop a strong sense of competency. This is when we need to feel like we can handle tasks, learn from mistakes, and trust that we are good enough. It's important for us to understand that doing our best is what truly matters and that our efforts are appreciated, not just our successes. This phase is key for building self-confidence and resilience.

Erik Erikson refers to this as the "industry versus inferiority" stage. As we start school and take on more structured activities, we're constantly learning new skills and facing new challenges. When caregivers and teachers provide encouragement, support, and positive feedback, we feel capable and confident in our abilities. However, if we face constant criticism or unrealistic expectations, we might begin to feel inferior, leading to self-doubt.

Learning from mistakes plays a crucial role in this stage. We need to know that it's okay to fail and that mistakes are simply part of the learning process. Supportive caregivers and teachers who frame mistakes as growth opportunities help us develop resilience and a growth mindset. This approach empowers us to take on challenges with confidence, reinforcing our belief in our own abilities.

If we don't receive the recognition and support we need, we can develop negative beliefs about ourselves. We might start to feel incompetent, like a failure, or think we're not good enough. These feelings can lead to overwhelm and guilt for not meeting expectations. It's essential our caregivers ensure we feel capable and that our efforts are acknowledged. By doing so, they help us build a strong, positive self-image that will serve us well throughout life.

Lucas's Story

Lucas, a 40-year-old software developer at a tech startup, came to me feeling paralyzed by a persistent sense of self-doubt and fear of making mistakes. Despite being highly skilled and respected by his colleagues, Lucas often second-guessed himself, fearing that one small error would unravel his entire reputation. He struggled with perfectionism at work, frequently overworking himself to avoid even the slightest mistake, which left him mentally exhausted and anxious. His fear of failure also impacted his personal life, where he hesitated to take risks or try new things, worried that he wouldn't be good enough.

In team settings at work, Lucas often found himself unable to delegate tasks or trust that his colleagues would handle things correctly. He felt it was safer to do everything himself, convinced that even a minor slip-up would reflect poorly on him. This pressure led him to micromanage projects, causing frustration both for himself and for his team. He also avoided asking for help or admitting when he didn't know something, fearing it would expose his inadequacies. As a result, Lucas often felt isolated, believing he had to carry the weight of everything on his own to avoid disappointing others or himself.

The root of Lucas's fear of making mistakes and his struggle with self-doubt could be traced back to his early years. One day, Lucas came home proudly waving a test he had aced with a score of 98%. Expecting praise, he instead heard his parents ask, "What happened to the other two points?" This question planted the seed in Lucas's mind that anything less than perfection wasn't good enough. His parents simply wanted him to reach his full potential, but their focus on his small errors left Lucas feeling that his accomplishments were never fully recognized. Over time, he internalized the belief that unless he was flawless, he wasn't worthy of praise or approval.

As Lucas grew older, this pressure to be perfect only intensified. In school, he worked hard to maintain top grades and never gave himself permission to make mistakes. He avoided subjects or activities where he felt he might struggle, preferring to stick to areas where he could excel and avoid any risk of failure. Though his teachers and peers saw him as a high achiever, Lucas never felt satisfied with his successes. He had a hard time internalizing his accomplishments, focusing instead on what he could have improved. This fear of imperfection carried into adulthood, leading Lucas to avoid challenges where he might fall short, reinforcing his belief that he wasn't good enough.

At work, Lucas's greatest strength was also his biggest weakness. While he was meticulous and thorough, his constant fear of making mistakes meant he took longer than necessary on tasks, fearing that even a small oversight would damage his credibility. When things didn't go according to plan, Lucas felt a deep sense of guilt and inadequacy, blaming himself for not living up to expectations. These feelings became a vicious cycle, as his fear of failure and self-doubt made it harder for him to bounce back from setbacks.

Eventually, the pressure Lucas placed on himself became too much to bear, and he sought therapy to try to understand why he felt so incapable, even when he was performing well. During our sessions, we explored the roots of his perfectionism and fear of making mistakes. Together, we traced these feelings back to that moment when his parents' seemingly harmless comment about the missing two points on his test made him believe that anything less than perfect wasn't enough. We also looked at how other experiences throughout his childhood reinforced this belief, such as being praised only for his successes and feeling like his mistakes were a direct reflection of his worth.

As Lucas began to understand the origins of his perfectionism, we worked on strategies to help him challenge these deeply ingrained beliefs. He learned techniques to reframe his thoughts around mistakes, seeing them not as failures but as opportunities for growth and learning. We also focused on self-compassion, encouraging Lucas to be kinder to himself when he made errors, rather than spiraling into guilt and self-criticism. Little by little, Lucas started to practice letting go of the need to be perfect, delegating tasks at work and allowing himself to make mistakes without feeling like his self-worth was at stake.

Though it was challenging at first, Lucas began to notice changes. He became more resilient in the face of setbacks, learning to recover more quickly when things didn't go as he had hoped. In his personal life, Lucas found that taking small risks, such as trying new hobbies or admitting when he needed help, didn't lead to the failure he feared. At work, he started to trust his colleagues more, realizing that collaboration often led to better results than trying to do everything himself.

Ages 7+: Vulnerability & Judgment

From age 7 onward, we enter a crucial stage where understanding and managing vulnerability becomes key. This period is about learning how to protect ourselves, trust our own judgment, and accept our unique qualities while still thriving. It's the time for us to recognize what we can control and to develop strategies for handling what we can't. Feeling empowered and capable of navigating life's challenges helps build our sense of security and self-confidence.

During this phase, Erik Erikson's "industry versus inferiority" concept still applies, but it gradually shifts toward "identity versus role confusion" as we move into adolescence. At this stage, we are not only refining our skills but also exploring who we are. We need supportive environments where we can express ourselves, make decisions, and sometimes fail without facing harsh consequences. These experiences teach us to trust our own judgment and build resilience, helping us avoid feeling overly vulnerable or powerless.

As we grow, we also start to embrace our individual differences. Positive reinforcement from caregivers and encouragement from peers play a significant role in this process. It's essential for us to feel that our uniqueness is valued and that we can succeed, no matter how different we may be. When we feel accepted and supported, we develop a strong sense of identity and are better equipped to handle vulnerability and uncertainty.

However, without the necessary support during this stage, we may begin to feel vulnerable, powerless, or helpless, believing we can't trust our own judgment. These feelings can trap us in self-doubt, making it harder for us to cope with life's challenges. By providing the tools and support to help us protect ourselves, make sound decisions, and embrace our differences, caregivers lay the foundation for a resilient mindset. This foundation allows us to face life's complexities with confidence, self-worth, and a strong sense of who we are.

Aisha's Story

Aisha, a 40-year-old communications manager at a nonprofit, had long known she needed therapy but avoided it, fearing the vulnerability it required. The idea of opening up emotionally felt overwhelming, and she worried it would make her feel exposed and powerless. Meanwhile, her self-doubt and fear of judgment steadily eroded her confidence, yet she convinced herself that vulnerability—even in a therapeutic setting—was too risky.

Eventually, the pressure became unmanageable. At work, Aisha hesitated to make decisions or share her opinions, despite being respected for her professionalism. She second-guessed herself constantly, fearing even minor mistakes would lead to judgment or criticism. This fear stifled her voice in meetings, where she often stayed silent, even when she had valuable ideas. Her self-doubt extended into her personal life as well, where she kept her emotions tightly guarded, avoiding deeper connections with loved ones to protect herself from feeling exposed.

The roots of Aisha's fear of vulnerability could be traced to her childhood. In 5th grade, she became the target of bullying, with classmates mocking her clothes, personality, and uniqueness. To shield herself, Aisha withdrew, suppressing her true self to avoid further ridicule. This coping mechanism provided safety at the time but left a lasting belief that being vulnerable would only lead to pain. As she grew older, this belief deepened. In high school and beyond, Aisha stayed under the radar, carefully managing her behavior to avoid standing out and keeping others at a distance.

In adulthood, these fears held her back professionally and personally. Aisha's fear of judgment caused her to overanalyze decisions and avoid leadership roles, even when she was highly capable. Any small mistake triggered feelings of inadequacy, reinforcing her reluctance to step into more visible positions. Personally, she avoided emotional openness with friends and family, keeping her guard up and limiting her ability to form deeper relationships.

When Aisha finally sought therapy, we explored how her childhood bullying had shaped her fear of judgment and vulnerability. We discussed how hiding her uniqueness had been a protective strategy as a child but now hindered her ability to live authentically. Together, we worked on strategies to manage vulnerability, including practicing decision-making without overthinking, trusting her instincts, and tolerating the discomfort of being open. Gradually, Aisha began to challenge her fears and test new behaviors.

Over time, she noticed significant changes. At work, Aisha started speaking up in meetings and confidently sharing her ideas, earning appreciation from colleagues who valued her perspective. This helped her see that being vulnerable didn't mean being powerless. In her personal life, she began opening up to loved ones, allowing for deeper connections and feeling relief as she realized she didn't have to guard herself constantly.

Adolescence & Adulthood

Erik Erikson's stages of development don't stop at childhood—they continue to shape us throughout adolescence and into adulthood, offering a roadmap for our ongoing growth and evolution.

In adolescence, roughly from ages 12 to 18, we enter the "identity versus role confusion" stage. This is when we start grappling with the big questions about who we are and where we fit in the world. We experiment with different roles, values, and beliefs, trying to figure out what resonates. Successfully navigating this stage helps us emerge with a strong sense of identity and the ability to stay true to ourselves and our ideals.

If we struggle, however, we may feel uncertain about our place in the world, which can lead to confusion and unstable relationships.

As we transition into young adulthood, from around 18 to 40, the focus shifts to "intimacy versus isolation." The challenge here is forming deep, meaningful relationships. Those who successfully navigate this stage build strong emotional connections and experience love and companionship. However, if we have difficulty, we may end up feeling lonely and isolated, finding it hard to form lasting bonds with others.

In middle adulthood, roughly from ages 40 to 65, we face the stage of "generativity versus stagnation." This is when we seek to make a lasting impact on the world—whether through raising children, excelling in our careers, or contributing to our communities. Successfully navigating this stage helps us feel productive and fulfilled, knowing we're leaving a positive mark on the world. If we struggle, though, we may feel stuck or disconnected, with a sense of stagnation and dissatisfaction.

Finally, in late adulthood, from age 65 onwards, we enter the stage of "integrity versus despair." At this point, life is about reflection. If we can look back with satisfaction, feeling that we've lived well and done what we set out to do, we achieve a sense of integrity and wisdom. On the other hand, if our reflections are filled with regret, we may experience despair, struggling with bitterness and feelings of missed opportunities.

Erikson's stages remind us that growth is a lifelong journey, with each phase building on the last. As we move through these stages, we have the opportunity to evolve, become more complete, and ultimately, more content individuals.

Discovery Prompt: Uncovering a Core Belief

Take 5-10 minutes to reflect on a recent emotional challenge. By repeatedly asking yourself, "What does this say about me?" or "What does this mean?" you can uncover core beliefs that influence your emotional reactions. Look at the example and then follow these steps:

1. **Identify a recent emotional event**: Think of a situation in which you experienced a strong emotion (e.g., frustration, anxiety, sadness). Briefly describe what happened and how you felt.

2. **Ask, "What does this say about me?"**: Reflect on why you reacted this way. What does it suggest about how you see yourself or others?

3. **Keep asking, "What does that mean?"**: Keep digging with this question until you reach a deeper understanding or belief.

4. **Recall an earlier memory**: Think back to your childhood when you felt a similar emotional reaction. What does this remind you of?

5. **Identify the core belief**: Based on your reflections, what core belief about yourself or the world might be driving your response?

<u>Example:</u>

Event: "I felt frustrated when a colleague dismissed my idea during a meeting."

What does that say about me? "It makes me feel like my input doesn't matter."

What does that mean? "It suggests that if people don't accept my ideas, they don't respect me."

What does that say about me? "It means I tie my self-worth to other people's approval."

What does that mean? "It suggests that being professionally rejected feels like a reflection of my personal value."

Earliest memory: "When I was 7, I remember showing my drawing to my dad, and he pointed out something I did wrong instead of praising it. I felt crushed and believed I had failed to meet his expectations."

Core belief: "If I don't receive external validation, it means I'm not good enough."

This exercise helps link your current emotional triggers to the core beliefs formed in childhood, revealing patterns that may shape your adult behavior and emotional responses.

CHAPTER 3

Inner Dialogues

Our core beliefs shape how we see the world and how we show up in it, affecting everything from our self-esteem to our relationships and careers. In this chapter, we're diving deep into some of the most common core beliefs and how they show up in our daily lives. We'll unpack the belief "my needs aren't important" and how it impacts both personal and professional life, explore the weight of feeling like "a disappointment," and tackle the effects of toxic shame, self-abandonment, the harsh inner critic, and interpersonal anxiety.

Believing that "my needs aren't important" often begins in childhood, setting the stage for a lifetime of putting others first while neglecting ourselves. This shows up as self-sacrifice—always giving, but feeling unappreciated and burnt out. Or maybe it's staying quiet at work, even though you're contributing a lot, but no one sees it. Not asking for help? That's part of it too, and it leads to stress, isolation, and feeling like you're carrying the weight of the world alone. These patterns chip away at your well-being.

Then there's the belief that you're "a disappointment." This one can cut deep, making you feel like you're always falling short of other people's expectations. It eats away at your self-worth and strains relationships. You might be constantly striving for approval, which leads to burnout, or second-guessing every career decision, even doubting your achievements. It's exhausting to always feel like you're not doing enough, driving you to seek validation over and over again.

But it's not just these specific beliefs. Toxic shame makes you feel disconnected and worthless. Self-abandonment shows up as people-pleasing and codependency, putting everyone else's needs before your own. The harsh inner critic, often born from childhood experiences, keeps you locked in a cycle of self-doubt and self-hatred. And interpersonal anxiety? That can make you overly independent, struggling to form real, deep connections with others.

By understanding how these beliefs shape our behavior, we can start to untangle the mess. It's all connected, and once you see the link, you can start making changes.

One Belief, Multiple Outcomes

My Needs aren't Important

Let's dive into the core belief: "*my needs aren't important.*" This belief often takes root early in life and can quietly but powerfully influence how we navigate both our personal and professional worlds. When someone believes their needs don't matter, it impacts how they relate to others, how they set boundaries, and how they see their own self-worth. To better understand this, let's explore the stories of Maria, James, and Priya - each facing unique challenges because of this belief.

Vignette 1: Maria's Self-Sacrifice

Maria, a 42-year-old nurse, is the epitome of dedication and selflessness. At work, she's the go-to person for covering extra shifts and always steps in to help her colleagues. But despite her long hours and relentless effort, Maria often feels unappreciated and overlooked.

Her core belief—that her needs aren't important—began in childhood. Growing up in a large family, Maria was expected to care for her younger siblings, often without acknowledgment or appreciation from her overwhelmed parents. She internalized the idea that her needs were secondary, and that her worth came from prioritizing others.

In her personal life, this belief manifests in her relationships. Maria rarely speaks up about her own desires or preferences, fearing she'll come across as selfish. In romantic relationships, she becomes overly accommodating, neglecting her own well-being to keep her partner happy. This pattern inevitably leads to burnout and resentment, further reinforcing her belief that her needs just don't matter.

Vignette 2: James's Workplace Silence

James, a 35-year-old software developer, is known for his quiet and unassuming nature. During meetings, even when he has valuable ideas, James rarely speaks up. He frequently takes on extra tasks without complaint, believing his role is to support the team, not seek recognition or assistance.

James's belief—that his needs aren't important—stems from his upbringing. As the middle child in a family that prioritized academic and athletic achievements, James always felt overshadowed by his siblings. His parents, though loving, were more focused on his siblings' accomplishments, leaving him to feel that his needs and successes were less significant.

This belief seeps into James's personal life as well. In his friendships, he often takes on the role of listener, rarely sharing his own struggles or asking for help. While his friends appreciate his empathy, James feels disconnected and unseen, which further reinforces his belief that his needs don't matter.

Vignette 3: Priya's Reluctance to Seek Help

Priya, a 29-year-old marketing executive, is viewed as highly competent and reliable by her colleagues. She tackles challenging projects head-on and works late into the night to ensure perfection. However, Priya struggles with asking for help or delegating tasks, believing that her needs for support aren't important.

Priya's belief took shape during her teenage years. Her parents, successful professionals themselves, held high expectations for her. While they provided well for her materially, they were emotionally distant and emphasized self-reliance. Priya learned early on that expressing her needs would disappoint them or make her seem weak.

In her personal life, Priya's reluctance to seek help affects her relationships. She often feels overwhelmed and stressed but hides these feelings from her friends and family. This sense of isolation only reinforces her belief that her needs aren't important. Priya carries the self-sabotaging belief that asking for support is a sign of weakness.

In each of these stories, the belief that "*my needs aren't important*" came from a different origin story, but ultimately led to burnout, self-doubt, and emotional neglect. By acknowledging this belief and recognizing how it plays out in their lives, Maria, James, and

Priya have the opportunity to rewrite their narratives—embracing self-worth, setting boundaries, and allowing themselves to ask for what they truly need.

I'm a Disappointment

The belief that "I'm not living up to others' expectations" or "I'm a disappointment" can profoundly shape a person's sense of self-worth and strain their relationships. Often rooted in early experiences, this belief influences how individuals view themselves and how they interact with others. Let's take a closer look at the personal stories of Sophie, Ethan, and Nikhil, who each face unique struggles tied to this belief.

Vignette 1: Sophie's Relentless Striving

Sophie, a 38-year-old attorney, feels like she's constantly falling short of her family's expectations. Despite her thriving career, she believes she's a disappointment for not following her parents into medicine. Growing up, her parents frequently compared her to her siblings, who all pursued careers in healthcare. These comparisons left Sophie feeling inferior and driven to overachieve in her own field.

Professionally, Sophie takes on more cases than she can handle, hoping that her relentless work ethic will earn her the approval she craves. She sacrifices her personal time, often skipping social events and neglecting her own well-being just to meet the impossible standards she's set for herself. Despite her success, Sophie finds little joy in her accomplishments, always feeling that she's falling short of what her family truly wants from her.

In her personal life, this constant striving leaves her exhausted and disconnected. She rarely finds time to engage in activities she enjoys or to simply relax. Her relationships with friends and family suffer as she struggles to balance work and life, leading to an overwhelming sense of isolation. Sophie's journey involves learning to set boundaries and recognize that her worth isn't tied to meeting anyone else's expectations but her own.

Vignette 2: Ethan's Career Choice

Ethan, a 29-year-old illustrator, feels crushed under the weight of his parents' expectations. They had envisioned a prestigious career for him, but Ethan chose to pursue his passion for drawing. While he loves his work, Ethan constantly fears that his choice disappointed his family, who had hoped he'd take a more traditional career path.

At work, Ethan excels and receives praise from his colleagues, but he struggles to share his successes with his family. He's convinced that his achievements seem insignificant compared to what his parents had envisioned for him. This self-doubt clouds his confidence and makes him hesitant to fully embrace new opportunities in his field.

Socially, Ethan often feels inadequate, worrying that others judge him for not meeting the more conventional standards of success. He finds it difficult to fully enjoy his accomplishments, as he constantly compares himself to peers who followed more traditional paths. Ethan's journey involves embracing his unique talents and learning to value his accomplishments, without needing his family's approval to feel validated.

Vignette 3: Nikhil's Familial Expectations

Nikhil, a 45-year-old project manager, has spent much of his life feeling like a disappointment to his father, who had hoped he would take over the family business. Instead, Nikhil followed his own passion into corporate management. His father's ongoing expressions of disappointment deeply impacted Nikhil, leaving him feeling like a failure for not living up to those expectations.

In his career, Nikhil is overly cautious, avoiding risks for fear that any mistake will confirm his belief that he's not good enough. He often shies away from pursuing innovative projects, worried that failure will diminish his self-worth even further. Despite his many achievements, Nikhil struggles to take pride in his work, constantly feeling as though it will never be enough in his father's eyes.

This belief also affects Nikhil's relationships, as he rarely opens up about his struggles, fearing judgment or further disappointment. He feels emotionally disconnected from his family and friends, who see him as successful but don't understand the internal battle he faces. Nikhil's journey is about learning to embrace his own path, recognizing his accomplishments, and realizing that his worth isn't determined by his father's approval.

Each of these stories—whether it's Sophie's need for validation through overachievement, Ethan's struggle to find pride in his unique path, or Nikhil's fear of never being enough—highlights the deep impact of believing we're a disappointment. But their stories also show that by recognizing and challenging these beliefs, they can begin to create a more self-assured and authentic sense of self.

Self-Schemas

Self-schemas are the mental frameworks we create based on our beliefs and experiences about who we are. These schemas, shaped by our upbringing, relationships, personal experiences, and societal influences, help guide how we think, feel, and act in various situations. They're deeply individualized, covering everything from behaviors and personality traits to physical characteristics and interests. For instance, one person might see themselves as shy, while others might view themselves as assertive, friendly, or artistic. Together, these self-schemas contribute to our overall self-concept—the complex image we hold of who we believe we are.

These schemas aren't fixed; they're dynamic and can change as we gain new experiences or feedback from others. They influence how we perceive and interact with the world, affecting everything from how we perform in different areas of life to how we approach relationships. For example, someone who views themselves as independent may thrive in situations requiring self-reliance, while negative self-schemas, like seeing oneself as incompetent, can hinder progress and create self-doubt. Understanding and improving self-schemas can be a powerful tool for personal development, fostering a more positive self-image and improving overall mental health.

Take the example of someone who sees themselves as a "*perfectionist.*" This self-schema, shaped by feedback from parents, teachers, and peers, leads them to set extremely high standards. At work or school, this belief compels them to spend extra time ensuring every detail is flawless, often at the expense of their own well-being. This perfectionist mindset doesn't just affect their work—it spills over into their relationships, causing frustration when others don't share the same meticulous standards. In the long run, this can lead to stress, burnout, and strained interactions with colleagues or loved ones.

Often, we operate on autopilot, reacting to situations without much thought. A trigger happens, we respond automatically, and only later might we reflect on our actions. But there's a more mindful way to engage with the world—by pausing and becoming aware of what's happening between the trigger and our reaction. Our reaction has less to do with the trigger and way more to do with our self-schema and core beliefs. Practicing self-awareness allows us to choose how we respond, leading to better decisions and more meaningful actions. Many times, we react quickly not because of the actual event, but because of the uncomfortable emotions it stirs up.

Toxic Shame

Toxic shame is a deep, lingering emotion that goes far beyond the passing feelings of guilt or embarrassment we all experience from time to time. While regular shame or guilt can motivate us to grow and foster connection, toxic shame is destructive. It usually begins in childhood, triggered by negative interactions with caregivers—such as indifference, disapproval, anger, or abandonment. Rather than feeling bad about specific actions, people who carry toxic shame believe that something is fundamentally wrong with them.

For those affected, toxic shame is like a heavy weight, constantly reinforcing the belief that they're flawed, worthless, and unlovable. It creates an overwhelming sense of disconnection, almost like physical pain. When children don't receive the emotional repair they need after these negative interactions, they often grow into anxious, avoidant adults who struggle with self-regulation and forming healthy relationships. Their nervous system stays in a constant state of high alert, making it difficult to feel safe, secure, or at ease.

People living with toxic shame often feel like they're failing at life. They may withdraw from social situations or get into relationships that reinforce their negative self-image. Constantly expecting rejection or failure only deepens the damage to their self-esteem, leaving them feeling isolated and disconnected. Avoiding eye contact, freezing in social situations, hiding their true selves, and fearing judgment are common behaviors for those caught in the grip of toxic shame.

Living with this form of shame makes it incredibly difficult to build healthy self-esteem, often leading to anxiety and depression. It also creates barriers to forming meaningful connections, as the fear of being seen as unlovable or defective keeps people from opening up or fully engaging with others. Overcoming toxic shame requires addressing these deeply ingrained beliefs and finding a safe space for emotional healing, such as therapy.

Inner Critic

The harsh inner critic many of us battle today often originates from the messages we absorbed as kids. When a child is constantly criticized, judged, or shamed, those external voices gradually become part of their internal dialogue. Over time, these negative attitudes shape how we view ourselves, leading to deep feelings of shame, guilt, and negative self-talk, which makes it difficult to cultivate a positive self-image.

This inner critic can also emerge from the struggle to earn love and approval from a parent or caregiver. As children, when self-criticism doesn't bring the approval we seek, the critical voice only gets louder, amplifying feelings of self-doubt and inadequacy. This makes it even harder to be kind to ourselves, as we become trapped in a cycle of trying to please others while hiding our true selves to avoid rejection or disappointment. If we grew up in an environment where our emotions were frequently dismissed or invalidated, we may have learned to silence our feelings and rely on self-criticism as a way to keep ourselves in check and attempt to protect ourselves from further emotional pain.

Living with a relentless inner critic looks like constant self-loathing, a fixation on worst-case scenarios, expecting failure, and striving for perfection. Many people believe that this internal criticism is necessary for success, but it actually erodes our well-being. When we criticize ourselves, our body's defense system responds by releasing stress hormones like cortisol and adrenaline. While this response is meant to protect us from physical threats, it turns inward, attacking our sense of self-worth. It's like our brain is stuck in fight-or-flight mode, even though the "threat" is coming from within.

This self-attack leads to chronic stress, anxiety, and even depression, while also interfering with the body's ability to heal and recover. For those who grew up in environments filled with negativity or invalidation, the inner critic can feel so ingrained that it becomes indistinguishable from our sense of identity. The critic becomes an internalized voice that's difficult to silence.

To quiet this harsh inner voice, we first need to recognize where it comes from and understand that it once served as a coping mechanism. Replacing self-criticism with self-compassion is key. By shifting our inner dialogue from harsh judgment to kindness, we begin to break the cycle of negative self-talk and embrace the care and validation we've always deserved.

Interpersonal Anxiety

Interpersonal anxiety often begins when we grow up without feeling safe, loved, or accepted. Without these essential foundations, we become reluctant to seek support from others, and as a way to cope, we may adopt self-sufficiency or hyper-independence as survival strategies. This means we start relying heavily on ourselves, avoiding vulnerability, and fearing that others may not show up when we need them.

In homes where we don't feel emotionally safe, we might learn to become someone we think others will love and accept. This is known as *impression management*—a way of coping in a critical, chaotic, or unpredictable environment. When we're constantly trying to please others or avoid conflict, showing our true selves feels risky, even terrifying.

Living with social anxiety can be exhausting. We're always scanning for how others are feeling, adapting to fit in, and managing our actions to avoid judgment. Social settings become stressful, leading to behaviors like overexplaining, second-guessing, and replaying conversations, worrying we've said something wrong. The fear of rejection or abandonment makes it hard to build meaningful, genuine connections.

Hyper-independence can also make it tough to trust others. We might view people as unreliable or unsafe, and therefore avoid leaning on them for comfort or support. People with interpersonal anxiety often excel in structured, goal-oriented environments where expectations are clear. However, they feel anxious and uneasy in unstructured social situations, where the "rules" are less defined, making them feel exposed.

To move beyond this anxiety, we need to start trusting others—bit by bit. It involves showing more of our true selves incrementally, taking small steps to open up, and finding security in relationships that are mutually respectful and allow us to be authentic. This process is gradual, but learning to trust and connect on a deeper level is key to overcoming the fear of rejection and building stronger, more fulfilling relationships.

Michael's Story

Michael, a 52-year-old financial analyst, built a reputation for his meticulous attention to detail and reliability at work. However, beneath his professional success lay a deep-seated struggle with interpersonal anxiety. Growing up in a turbulent household where his parents frequently argued and often neglected his emotional needs, Michael never felt truly safe, loved, or accepted. This lack of security in his formative years led him to adopt hyper-independence as a survival strategy. He learned to rely heavily on himself, avoiding dependence on others out of fear that they might let him down when he needed them most.

Michael's hyper-independence can be traced back to specific moments in his childhood that cemented his belief that relying on others was unsafe. He vividly remembers a night when, at just eight years old, he waited anxiously for his father to come home after promising to attend his school play—only for his father to forget entirely amid another explosive argument with his mother. That crushing disappointment wasn't an isolated event but part of a pattern that taught Michael to expect emotional letdowns from those closest to him. Over time, these experiences hardened into a belief that he could only depend on himself. This mindset, though protective in his youth, eventually isolated him in adulthood, where his carefully controlled independence masked a deep yearning for connection—a conflict that left him feeling both self-reliant and profoundly alone.

Throughout his childhood, Michael found solace in academic achievement and solitary activities. At school, he became the "perfect student," excelling in his studies and avoiding trouble by keeping to himself. At home, the chaos and unpredictability forced him to develop a keen sense of impression management. He constantly monitored his parents' moods and adjusted his behavior to avoid conflict, striving to be the son they would approve of, even if it meant suppressing his true self. This coping mechanism followed him into adulthood, where he continued to mold his personality to fit the expectations of those around him.

In social settings, Michael's interpersonal anxiety became particularly pronounced. He often found himself overexplaining his actions, doubting his words, and replaying conversations in his head, worrying that he might have said something wrong. The fear of rejection and abandonment made it difficult for him to connect with others on a deeper level. Instead of enjoying social interactions, Michael constantly felt the pressure to perform and please, making these experiences incredibly stressful. As a result, he tended to avoid unstructured social situations where the "rules" were less defined and he felt out of control, which further reinforced his belief systems.

Michael's hyper-independence made it challenging for him to trust others. He viewed people as unreliable sources of comfort, preferring the predictability of structured, goal-oriented environments like his workplace, where expectations are clear. However, this self-imposed isolation took a toll on his emotional well-being. Despite his professional accomplishments, Michael felt a persistent emptiness and longed for genuine connections.

His path to healing involved confronting the very beliefs that kept him emotionally isolated. We explored how his childhood experiences had shaped his fear of relying on others and began challenging the idea that vulnerability equals dependence. He worked on taking small, deliberate steps—like sharing personal thoughts with a trusted colleague or asking a friend for support during a difficult time—to test the waters of emotional connection. Over time, Michael realized that true strength didn't come from self-reliance alone but from the courage to let others in. By embracing this process, he was able to build deeper, more meaningful relationships where he felt valued not just for what he could do, but for his authentic self.

Filtering Information Through the Lenses of our Core Beliefs

When we encounter new information, our brain naturally tries to fit it into a mental framework we've built over time. We tend to focus on details that reinforce our beliefs and ignore those that don't. For instance, if someone believes the world is a hostile place, they'll notice and remember news about crime or conflict far more than acts of kindness. On the flip side, positive events that don't fit their worldview may get overlooked or dismissed.

This filtering process strengthens our core beliefs, creating a cycle where our perception of reality continually supports these views, even when they're based on incomplete or biased information. Over time, this selective perception can limit our understanding, trapping us within the boundaries of our mental framework and making it harder to grow or see things differently.

However, recognizing this process is empowering. By becoming aware of how we filter information, we can start to challenge and reassess our core beliefs. This self-awareness opens us up to new perspectives and experiences, leading to a more balanced and nuanced understanding of the world. It fosters greater empathy, flexibility, and personal growth.

Take Jake, for example. A 34-year-old graphic designer, Jake always viewed the world through the lens of his core belief that he was unlovable. This belief acted like a pair of dark glasses, coloring every interaction. When he walked into the office and saw colleagues laughing, he assumed they were talking about him, reinforcing his belief that he wasn't liked. If a client wasn't thrilled with a design, he blamed himself, using it as proof that he wasn't good enough.

One day, after a project meeting, a long-term client approached Jake to personally thank him for his exceptional work. Despite the sincere gratitude, Jake's internal filter dismissed the compliment as politeness rather than genuine appreciation. Later, when a colleague praised his creativity, he shrugged it off, thinking they were just being nice. His brain latched onto any hint of rejection or criticism while positive feedback slid away, barely acknowledged.

Jake's selective perception trapped him in a cycle where his belief in his unlovability was constantly reinforced, making it hard for him to see himself as others did: a talented, creative, and valued designer appreciated by both clients and colleagues.

By recognizing this pattern, Jake could begin challenging his core belief, opening himself to the reality that he *was* seen, valued, and loved by those around him. This shift in perspective was the first step toward a healthier self-image.

Discovery Prompt:
Understanding Your Inner Critic

This exercise is designed to help you pinpoint your inner critic, figure out where it's coming from, and start shifting toward a more compassionate inner voice. After looking at the example, take 5-10 minutes to walk through the steps below:

1. **Identify a recent moment when you were hard on yourself:** Think back to a time when you beat yourself up. What happened, and what specific things did your inner voice say? Jot down the words or judgments that came up.

2. **Ask yourself, "Whose voice is this?":** Does this critical voice sound like yours, or does it remind you of someone from your past—maybe a parent, sibling, or teacher? Did you hear similar things growing up? Write down any connections you notice.

3. **Challenge that inner critic:** Take each harsh thought and ask, "Is this 100% true?" or "Would I ever say this to a friend?" Then, write down a more balanced or compassionate response for each one.

4. **Recall an early memory of feeling this way:** Can you think back to a time in childhood when you felt similarly criticized or judged? Write down that memory and how it felt.

5. **Reframe it with compassion:** Imagine speaking to your younger self in that moment. What would you say to reassure or comfort them? Write a response that focuses on kindness and understanding.

Example:

Moment of self-criticism: "I looked in the mirror this morning and thought, 'I'm so out of shape. I'm going to look like a cow next to my friends on this girls' trip we have coming up next month."

Whose voice is this?: "It feels like the comments my older sister used to make about my body growing up, always putting me down."

Challenging the critic: "Is this true? No, my worth doesn't depend on how I look. Everyone's body is different, and I deserve to feel good about myself as I am."

Earliest memory: "I was 12 at a family event when a relative said, 'You'd be so pretty if you lost a little weight.' I felt ashamed, like my worth was tied to how thin I was."

Reframing with compassion: "To my younger self: You're beautiful just as you are. Your value isn't tied to your appearance or weight, and it's okay to be exactly who you are."

By getting to the root of your inner critic and speaking to yourself with more kindness, you can start breaking that cycle of negative self-talk and build a stronger, more compassionate inner dialogue.

PART 2

SELF-SABOTAGE

In this section, we turn our focus to the ways our deep-seated beliefs can manifest as self-sabotaging behaviors, often without us even realizing it (remember those blind spots I mentioned?). When we cling to beliefs like *"I'm not good enough"* or *"I must be perfect to be valued,"* these thoughts can lead us to act in ways that undermine our own happiness and success.

These self-sabotaging behaviors—whether they show up as procrastination, perfectionism, or imposter syndrome—are often our mind's misguided way of protecting us from perceived emotional threats. While these behaviors may have served a purpose at some point, today they keep us trapped in cycles of doubt, fear, and frustration. By understanding how these behaviors are deeply rooted in our core beliefs, we can begin to see how we hold ourselves back from reaching our true potential.

Throughout this chapter, we'll explore the various ways these beliefs fuel self-sabotage. We'll examine how perfectionism can cause us to hide our goals from others out of fear of falling short, how imposter syndrome leads us to doubt our achievements and fear being "found out," and how procrastination is often about avoiding uncomfortable emotions rather than poor time management. Though these behaviors may seem different, they share a common thread: they are all driven by the stories we tell ourselves about who we are and what we deserve.

By recognizing these patterns, we can begin to challenge the limiting beliefs that drive them. This chapter is about shining a light on the ways we unknowingly get in our own way and offering a path forward—one where we can rewrite the narratives that no longer serve us and step into a more empowered, self-compassionate way of living.

I've categorized these self-sabotaging behaviors according to the developmental stages discussed in Chapter 2, along with examples of core beliefs that may have contributed to these patterns. While this list is not exhaustive, it highlights common themes I've encountered in my work as a therapist. There's significant overlap between the beliefs and behaviors, and one belief can lead to multiple self-sabotaging actions. Additionally, the beliefs and behaviors I've identified aren't limited to the categories I've placed them in—I've done this simply to make it easier for you to follow along.

CHAPTER 4

Belief Cluster – Survival & Existence

Core Beliefs:

- "I am abandoned and alone"
- "My needs don't matter"
- "I don't deserve to be loved"

Self-Sabotaging Behaviors:

- **Hypervigilance** – Driven by a need to stay safe and be hyper-aware of threats.

Note: Hypervigilance is based in our nervous system and is not necessarily a self-sabotaging response, as it was formed to ensure our safety & survival. That said, it is something we can work on changing through the use of emotional regulation techniques.

Survival, Hypervigilance, and the Struggle for Safety

The beliefs we carry as adults often trace back to the survival instincts we developed as children. When our basic needs for safety and connection were unmet or inconsistent, we absorbed subconscious narratives like: *I am unsafe. I am invisible. I don't matter. I am broken. I am unworthy. I am alone. I don't belong. I am always at risk.* These beliefs took root in environments that felt unpredictable or threatening, teaching us that survival required constant vigilance and adaptation.

In homes where caregivers were emotionally unavailable, volatile, or neglectful, many children took on roles far beyond their years to create a sense of stability. These "little adults" became experts at reading the room—attuned to every subtle shift in mood, every unspoken cue—whether it was a parent's looming outburst or the quiet withdrawal that signaled emotional abandonment. This hyperawareness was a survival strategy, allowing the child to anticipate and defuse potential danger.

As adults, these survival strategies show up as hypervigilance—a relentless state of alertness to threats, even when none exist. If your childhood taught you that safety depended on controlling your environment, you might find yourself constantly scanning for signs of trouble in your relationships, interactions, and surroundings. The underlying belief? Your well-being is always on the line, and it's up to you to keep things under control.

Living in this perpetual state of "on guard" takes a heavy toll. It might manifest as social anxiety, where even the simplest interactions feel loaded with risk. You might over analyze every facial expression, tone of voice, or offhand comment, searching for hidden danger or disapproval. This hyper-awareness, meant to protect you, often backfires—leaving you drained, disconnected, and stuck in a feedback loop of stress.

Hypervigilance also makes authenticity feel like a risk. Vulnerability becomes dangerous because it reminds you of those times when showing your true self didn't bring safety, love, or belonging. Instead, you may rely on perfectionism, people-pleasing, or emotional detachment to protect yourself. Relaxing, trusting others, or believing that you are enough—just as you are—can feel impossible.

Healing begins with recognizing that the danger you once faced is no longer your current reality. The survival strategies that helped you as a child are not failures—they were necessary adaptations. But now, they may be keeping you stuck in patterns that no longer serve you.

Rewriting these ingrained beliefs starts with small, intentional shifts:

- *I am safe now.*
- *My needs are valid, and I can meet them.*
- *I am worthy of love and connection as I am.*
- *It's safe to be vulnerable with people who've earned my trust.*
- *I can trust myself to navigate challenges.*

CHAPTER 5

Belief Cluster - Control

Core Beliefs:

- "I need to be in control"
- "I'm trapped and powerless"
- "I should have acted differently"

Self-Sabotaging Behaviors:

- **Control issues ("Type A")** – Reflects a need to maintain control to feel secure.
- **Conflict avoidance** – Used to prevent loss of control or chaotic situations.
- **Indecisiveness** – Stems from uncertainty in controlling one's environment or decisions.

Control Issues (Being "Type A")

Core beliefs can deeply shape our need for control, often driving behaviors that we might not immediately recognize as controlling. At its core, the desire to control is an attempt to create safety and predictability in our lives. When we feel uncertain or vulnerable, controlling our environment—or the people around us—can seem like the best way to protect ourselves from potential harm or disappointment. This need can show up in subtle ways, like being overly critical of how others do things or refusing help, even when we're overwhelmed.

For someone with a strong need for control, it can feel safer to take on everything yourself rather than rely on others. This often leads to a "Type A" personality, where perfectionism and high expectations drive us to do things a certain way—or not at all. When things don't go according to plan or when someone else's actions don't meet our standards, we might react by shutting down, giving the silent treatment, or even blaming others for our stress. These reactions are often rooted in the fear that if we let go of control, everything will fall apart.

This need for control also seeps into relationships, where it might manifest as keeping score, guilting others, or snooping to ensure everything is "right." These behaviors often come from a deep belief that if we don't keep everything in check, we'll be hurt, disappointed, or taken advantage of. The irony, of course, is that while controlling behaviors are meant to create safety and stability, they usually lead to tension, distance, and conflict in relationships—undermining the connection and support that's truly needed.

Ultimately, the need for control is a response to underlying fears and insecurities. By recognizing these core beliefs and how they impact our behavior, we can begin to let go of the need to control everything. Instead, we can work toward embracing a more flexible, trusting approach to life and relationships.

Conflict Avoidance

Core beliefs have a profound impact on how we handle conflict, often leading us to avoid it altogether. Many of us were raised to view conflict as something negative, a sign that something's wrong or broken. If this resonates with you, it might be because you were taught that expressing your feelings or needs—especially when they caused discomfort for others—was something to be ashamed of. This creates a deep-seated fear of conflict, where it feels like something to dodge at all costs rather than a natural and healthy part of life.

If you grew up in an environment where difficult emotions were discouraged or ignored, you may have learned to bottle them up rather than express them. Over time, this leads to a sense of loneliness and disconnection, as though your emotions are "too much" for others to handle. The belief that conflict should always be avoided, combined with the shame of "rocking the boat," can make you retreat from uncomfortable situations rather than face them.

As an adult, this pattern might show up in how you deal with your own emotions. Instead of sharing what you're feeling with those who care about you, you might try to figure everything out on your own, or worse, suppress your emotions altogether. This often leads to hiding parts of yourself and wondering why you feel lonely or out of touch. When you've bottled things up for too long, they can spill out at the wrong time—whether in an emotional outburst, shutting down, or even having a meltdown that catches you by surprise. This only reinforces feelings of frustration and disconnection.

The truth is, conflict is a natural and inevitable part of any relationship. When you start to see conflict not as something to fear but as an opportunity to grow, it can transform how you handle difficult situations. Embracing conflict helps you understand yourself and others more deeply, building emotional resilience and strengthening your relationships. By accepting that conflict is part of life, you can stop judging yourself for it, approach tough moments with curiosity, and handle them with compassion and creativity. Instead of running from conflict, you learn to face it in a way that brings greater understanding and connection.

Indecisiveness

Core beliefs can have a surprising impact on how decisive we are, often leading to a frustrating cycle of indecision. The key to overcoming this isn't necessarily about fixing the original cause of your indecisiveness, but recognizing that the habits you've developed now are what keep it going. As a therapist, I've seen many smart, thoughtful people struggle with indecision, and often the root of the problem is so simple it's easy to overlook.

One of the biggest habits that fuels indecisiveness is self-doubt. It's normal to have doubts when making decisions, but when you constantly second-guess yourself, that doubt snowballs into anxiety, leaving you stuck. The difference between decisive and indecisive people isn't the absence of doubt—it's about trusting yourself enough to make a decision anyway. Ironically, the only way to build that trust is to keep making decisions, even when you're unsure. The more you practice, the more confidence you build in your own judgment.

Another habit that feeds indecisiveness is *catastrophizing*—imagining the worst-case scenario every time you face a decision. This ramps up your anxiety, making it feel like the stakes are impossibly high. Your mind goes into overdrive, turning small concerns into full-blown disasters. Instead of getting stuck in that cycle, try to balance things out by imagining the best-case scenario as well. Giving equal mental space to both outcomes can provide some much needed flexibility and perspective.

People-pleasing also plays a huge role in indecisiveness. When you're constantly focused on what others want, you teach yourself that your own desires and decisions aren't as important. Over time, this undermines your confidence, making it even harder to decide what's right for you. A good first step in breaking this habit is to simply ask yourself what *you* want in a situation—even if you don't act on it immediately. The more you tune into your own needs and values, the easier it becomes to make decisions that feel authentic. A *full body yes* is that unmistakable feeling when everything in you—your gut, your heart, your whole being—lights up with certainty. It's like your body knows the answer before your mind does, guiding you toward what feels right and away from what doesn't.

Sometimes, the decisions we make are thoughtful and reflect the energy we want to bring into the world. But at other times, they're reactive, driven by external pressures or patterns we haven't fully examined. When life gets busy—whether you're starting a new job, recovering from an illness, or managing a hectic family schedule—it's easy to slip into autopilot decision-making.

You also need to keep in mind that very few decisions are irreversible. Many overthinkers assume every decision is permanent and that the wrong choice will lead to devastating consequences. This belief is often shaped by early experiences where mistakes were judged harshly, making failure feel catastrophic. But in reality, most decisions in life are like two-way doors—if you don't like the outcome, you can usually turn back or change course. Bold action, even if imperfect, creates valuable experience and lessons that will benefit you regardless of the result. The fear of making the wrong decision keeps people stuck, but the truth is, you can almost always course-correct along the way.

CHAPTER 6

Belief Cluster – Responsibility

Core Beliefs:

- "I must take care of everything or everyone"
- "I can't afford to fail or make mistakes"
- "I'm a disappointment"

Self-Sabotaging Behaviors:

- **Toxic productivity** – The belief that overwhelm equals success and feelings of guilt for not living up to expectations.
- **People pleasing & codependency** – Taking on responsibility for others' emotions, needing approval to feel in control.
- **Insecure overachievers** – Trying to meet responsibilities or expectations excessively to feel competent.

Toxic Productivity

If you feel guilty when you take a break or try to relax, you might be dealing with productivity anxiety. This pressure to always be productive is something many people experience, and it can lead to stress, self-doubt, and eventual burnout.

At the root of this issue are our core beliefs. If you believe your worth is tied to how much you accomplish, you'll push yourself relentlessly. This mindset sets the stage for chronic stress by pushing you to set impossible goals, fear mistakes, and endlessly compare yourself to others. Our "always dialed in" culture reinforces these beliefs and behaviors.

Recognizing productivity anxiety is the first step toward managing it. One sign is setting unrealistic goals for yourself, leaving no room for error. I see this happen a lot when clients schedule their entire day but don't leave any wiggle room for unforeseen interferences. Then they get down on themselves for not accomplishing everything they set out to accomplish that day. These high expectations often come from a core belief that you must be perfect to be valued. When you don't meet these goals, your anxiety spikes. Instead, try setting realistic goals that take your limits into account.

Another sign of productivity anxiety is constantly comparing yourself to others, which can erode self-esteem and make you feel inadequate. This habit stems from the belief that you're only worthy if you're outperforming those around you. Focusing on your own progress and achievements can help shift your perspective. It's about measuring your current self against where you've come from, not where you're going.

Feeling guilty about taking breaks is another common sign of productivity anxiety. If you worry that every second you're not working is time wasted, it's time to rethink that approach. Breaks are essential for maintaining long-term productivity, so set boundaries and make sure you're allowing time for rest. If you always feel like you're not doing enough, it might be because your standards are too high, driven by the belief that you must always be productive to be worthy. Be kind to yourself, celebrate your accomplishments, and adjust your expectations to be more realistic. Research shows that taking breaks actually leads to greater efficiency when you are working.

Productivity anxiety can also show up physically, through symptoms like tension headaches, muscle stiffness, or trouble sleeping. Instead of just treating the symptoms, set clear boundaries between work and personal time—like committing to not work after office hours. Mindfulness or meditation can help calm your mind and ease stress. Remember, it's okay to have off days and to not be productive all the time. We're not machines, and taking care of your mental and physical health is just as important as getting shit done.

People Pleasing & Codependency

Core beliefs play a significant role in why some of us become people-pleasers, also known as the fawn response. When we fawn, we consistently put others' needs ahead of our own in an attempt to avoid conflict, criticism, or disapproval. It's as though we believe we must sacrifice our own needs and boundaries to feel accepted and safe in relationships.

Much of this behavior stems from past impactful experiences in childhood. If you grew up in a household where you had to care for your parents or felt a lot of shame, you may have learned that keeping everyone else happy was the only way to feel valued. This pattern of behavior becomes a way of coping with the fear that if you don't please others, you'll face rejection or lose love.

The fawn response is particularly common in those who've experienced repeated relational trauma in close relationships, like with parents or caregivers. In such environments, putting others first became an emotional survival strategy. This can manifest in various ways—pursuing a career just to make your parents happy, always agreeing with others to avoid conflict, or constantly apologizing even when it's unnecessary.

These behaviors are fueled by a deep fear of rejection and the core belief that your worth is tied to making others happy. If you've grown up believing that you have to meet everyone else's needs to feel valued, you may end up neglecting your own needs in order to gain approval. Over time, this can lead to codependency, where your sense of self becomes entwined with taking care of others, even to your detriment.

This mindset makes setting healthy boundaries extremely difficult. If you believe you must always be available and helpful to be loved, saying no feels impossible. This creates a cycle where you constantly sacrifice your well-being to maintain relationships, leading to feelings of exhaustion, resentment, and a loss of identity. As your self-worth becomes increasingly tied to serving others, it becomes harder to know who you are without that role.

Codependency is closely linked to the fawn response, where people-pleasing becomes a way to avoid conflict and secure approval. This behavior is driven by core beliefs that prioritize harmony and acceptance over being true to oneself. You might find yourself bending over backward to keep others happy, avoiding confrontation at all costs, and doing whatever it takes to maintain peace. These actions reinforce the belief that your primary role is to serve and support others, perpetuating the cycle of codependency and fawning.

Feeling unworthy of love or believing you must earn affection through self-sacrifice can create a powerful lens through which you view relationships, which may drive you to seek out dynamics that confirm them, no matter how harmful. This can lead to a pattern of attracting partners with narcissistic traits, who exploit your need for validation, or partners who are emotionally or physically abusive, reinforcing the idea that love comes with pain or conditions. Without addressing these deep-seated beliefs, the cycle persists, leaving you stuck in unhealthy and destructive relationships.

Yasa's Story

Yasa, a 42-year-old HR manager, came to me feeling trapped in her relationship with her long-term partner. She described him as charismatic and confident but admitted that his narcissistic tendencies left her feeling drained, anxious, and questioning her worth. Yasa often found herself walking on eggshells, constantly striving to meet her partner's demands and avoid his criticism. Over time, her sense of self had diminished, and she felt like her identity had been consumed by her role in the relationship.

At home, Yasa felt responsible for maintaining peace, often bending over backward to avoid conflict. Her partner frequently dismissed her feelings and needs, prioritizing his own desires and expecting her to cater to them without question. When Yasa tried to assert herself, he would deflect by criticizing her or accusing her of being ungrateful, leaving her doubting her own perspective. Despite these dynamics, Yasa struggled to leave the relationship, believing that her role was to fix things and keep her partner happy. This pattern of self-sacrifice had left her exhausted, resentful, and disconnected from her own needs.

At work, Yasa's people-pleasing tendencies also took a toll. She found it difficult to set boundaries with colleagues and often took on tasks that others avoided, even when it meant staying late or sacrificing her personal time. Her fear of disappointing others made it hard for her to say no, which led to burnout. The stress of her work life combined with the emotional toll of her relationship left Yasa feeling like she was running on empty.

The roots of Yasa's codependency and people-pleasing behaviors could be traced back to her childhood. Growing up in a household where her father was domineering and her mother was emotionally distant, Yasa learned early on that the best way to avoid conflict and criticism was to be agreeable and meet others' expectations. When she expressed her feelings or needs, her father would dismiss her or belittle her, leaving her feeling invisible and unimportant. Her mother, while not overtly unkind, avoided confrontation and modeled the same self-sacrificing behavior, reinforcing Yasa's belief that love and approval were earned by keeping others happy.

One formative memory stood out in our sessions: at the age of nine, Yasa had worked hard to create a birthday card for her father, pouring her heart into every detail. Instead of acknowledging her effort, he pointed out a spelling error and asked why she hadn't done better. This seemingly small moment left a lasting impression, reinforcing Yasa's belief that her worth was tied to perfection and the approval of others. Over time, she internalized the idea that if she wasn't meeting others' expectations, she risked rejection or criticism.

As an adult, these early experiences shaped Yasa's approach to relationships. Her fear of conflict and desire to please made her vulnerable to partners who took advantage of her willingness to prioritize their needs over her own. Her current partner's narcissistic tendencies only exacerbated this dynamic, as he often used her fear of rejection to manipulate her into compliance. Yasa's sense of self-worth had become so entwined with keeping him happy that she struggled to recognize her own needs or assert her boundaries.

When Yasa finally sought me out for therapy, she admitted that she felt ashamed for needing help. She feared that opening up about her struggles would make her seem weak or needy. In our sessions, we began unpacking the core beliefs that had driven her people-pleasing tendencies. Together, we explored how her childhood experiences had shaped her fear of rejection and her belief that love and approval had to be earned through self-sacrifice.

Yasa started to challenge these deeply ingrained beliefs. She worked on recognizing and validating her own emotions, learning that her needs were just as important as those of others. We practiced setting small boundaries in manageable ways, such as saying no to non-essential tasks at work or expressing her preferences in low-stakes situations. Over time, Yasa built up the confidence to set clearer boundaries with her partner, recognizing that she didn't have to tolerate disrespect or manipulation to maintain the relationship.

Yasa also began to explore her sense of identity outside of her role as a caregiver and fixer. She reconnected with hobbies and interests she had abandoned, discovering joy in creative pursuits and spending time with supportive friends. By focusing on her own needs and desires, she began to rebuild her sense of self-worth, independent of her partner's approval.

Insecure Overachievers

Core beliefs play a crucial role in shaping someone into an insecure overachiever, a personality type that often overlaps significantly with perfectionism. These individuals are driven by a deep sense of inadequacy. For instance, if someone grew up feeling that their parents' love or approval was conditional on their performance, they may develop the belief that they must constantly prove their worth through achievements. This belief can also stem from experiences of financial or emotional deprivation, where success becomes synonymous with security, approval, and love.

Elite professional organizations, such as corporate law firms, often target insecure overachievers because of their relentless self-motivation and ambition. These firms understand that individuals driven by the need to prove themselves will go to extraordinary lengths, often working tirelessly to meet expectations. The message these organizations send is, "*We are the best, and because we want you, that makes you the best, too.*" This external validation temporarily boosts the insecure overachiever's self-esteem, reinforcing their core belief that their worth is directly tied to their professional success.

However, the reality inside these high-pressure environments can be harsh. Up-or-out policies and constant performance evaluations exacerbate the insecurities of overachievers, intensifying their fear of being exposed as inadequate. This perpetual anxiety pushes them to overwork, constantly striving to meet both their own impossibly high standards and those imposed by their employers. The core belief that they aren't inherently valuable drives them to seek validation through relentless achievement, creating a vicious cycle of stress, anxiety, and eventual burnout. Ironically, they often get into a self-imposed competition with themselves to outperform themselves.

As a result, the drive for perfection leaves little room for self-compassion or balance. Insecure overachievers often neglect their well-being, prioritizing work over everything else to avoid the devastating possibility of failure or rejection. This intense focus on professional success not only damages their mental and physical health but also strains personal relationships and leads to a lack of fulfillment outside their career. In the end, despite all their accomplishments, insecure overachievers are left feeling empty, trapped in a cycle where success never feels like enough.

CHAPTER 7

Belief Cluster – Worthiness

Core Beliefs:

- **"I'm worthless or not good enough"**
- **"Love depends on what I do, not who I am"**
- **"If I'm not perfect, I cannot accept myself"**

Self-Sabotaging Behaviors:

- **Perfectionism** – A fear of failure and feeling of unworthiness unless achieving perfect results.

- **Self-medicating** - Using substances or other numbing behaviors to cope with emotional pain and stress

- **Unrealistic expectations (of self & others)** – Aimed at proving competency but unrealistic and self-defeating.

- **Imposter Syndrome** – Feeling fraudulent and having difficulty internalizing success.

- **Overly critical (of self & others)** – Reflects feelings of unworthiness, often manifesting as self-criticism and projected onto others.

Perfectionism

Perfectionism might seem like a relentless drive for excellence, but at its core, it's often fueled by fear—particularly the fear of failure. Perfectionists can feel paralyzed by the thought of not achieving flawless results on the first try, leading to endless procrastination disguised as over-preparing or busywork. This fear not only wastes precious time but also keeps them stuck, avoiding challenges that could help them grow. It's a vicious cycle that prioritizes avoiding failure over pursuing meaningful progress.

At the heart of this pattern is a *fixed mindset* - the belief that abilities are static and mistakes expose inherent flaws. This mindset convinces perfectionists to avoid risks, shield themselves from critical feedback, and give up at the first sign of difficulty. In contrast, a *growth mindset* embraces challenges as opportunities to learn and views failure as a stepping stone rather than a dead end. The good news? Mindsets can change. With intentional effort, even the most entrenched perfectionists can rewire their approach, transforming fear into curiosity and unlocking their true potential.

Perfectionists often keep their goals and dreams to themselves, even from those closest to them, to avoid the sting of potential failure. For example, they might not mention an exciting opportunity or a potential promotion until it's a sure thing, out of fear of embarrassment if things don't go as planned. This behavior is rooted in a fear of failure, leading perfectionists to use defense mechanisms like hiding their true feelings to avoid vulnerability. It's like putting on a front of "everything's great" while feeling stressed or insecure on the inside, or keeping aspirations a secret to dodge further disappointment.

But this strategy tends to backfire. Research shows that social support can significantly boost motivation, resilience, and overall chances of success. By keeping dreams hidden, perfectionists miss out on the encouragement and guidance that could make all the difference. Plus, facing disappointment in isolation often makes it feel worse. Sharing setbacks with trusted friends and family can provide comfort, perspective, and a reminder that failure isn't the end of the world.

Even after major setbacks, relying on social support is crucial for bouncing back and viewing it as an opportunity for growth. While it's essential to maintain healthy boundaries and not overshare, letting in those who truly support us can be transformative. Disappointments are an inevitable part of life, but we don't have to face them alone. Opening up to the right people not only strengthens relationships but also helps us handle life's challenges with greater resilience and confidence.

Self-Medicating

When we turn to things like food, alcohol, drugs, endlessly scrolling through our phones, or binge-watching shows, what we're really doing is trying to numb ourselves. It's a way of avoiding the uncomfortable emotions or thoughts that feel too overwhelming to face. Rather than sitting with those feelings and working through them, we grab onto a quick distraction—a snack to ease the stress, a drink to drown out emotional pain, or social media to fill the loneliness. These actions might offer short-term relief, but they never actually solve the deeper issues that are lurking just below the surface. Instead, they let that pain build up, waiting for the next opportunity to burst back through.

What makes this cycle even more complicated is that these behaviors are often tied to our core beliefs. For example, someone who believes they're not good enough might turn to comfort food or alcohol to dull the sting of that belief. But instead of addressing the root cause—the belief itself—they're just slapping a bandage on it. And like any wound that needs stitches, ignoring it only makes it worse. The negative belief doesn't go away; it keeps simmering beneath the surface, and in many ways, we're actually reinforcing it by trying to avoid it. This is why the cycle keeps repeating. We're using temporary fixes for a problem that needs a more permanent solution.

What makes it all the more frustrating is that, on some level, we usually know these behaviors aren't helping. We're aware that grabbing a snack when we're not hungry or drinking to push down our feelings isn't the answer, yet we keep doing it. Why? It's not just about willpower. Often, it's our core beliefs that keep driving us toward these behaviors. If, deep down, we believe we're unworthy or incapable, no amount of "knowing better" will stop us from reaching for those distractions. It's like trying to build a house on a shaky foundation. No matter how much effort you put into it, it won't stand up until you fix the core issue beneath it.

This is where the cycle starts to look like self-sabotage. Instead of facing the root of our pain and dealing with it, we keep avoiding it, staying stuck in the same patterns that hold us back. By reaching for these quick fixes, we're not just avoiding pain—we're also keeping ourselves from moving forward. Every time we turn to another distraction, we're postponing the real work that needs to be done. And the more we avoid these emotions, the more disconnected we become from ourselves. Over time, these habits don't just numb our pain; they numb our ability to connect with who we really are, robbing us of the chance to live a more authentic, fulfilling life.

What's especially damaging is that the more we avoid these uncomfortable feelings, the more power they gain. We might think we're sidestepping the problem, but avoidance doesn't make the pain disappear—it magnifies it over time. The stress, sadness, and fear that we bury don't just vanish; they leak into other areas of our lives, often in ways we don't even realize.

And the longer we stay in this numbing cycle, the harder it becomes to break free. The distractions become a way of life, a kind of autopilot we slip into without even realizing it. But deep down, we know that avoiding these feelings isn't the way forward. The real work—the work that truly helps us heal and grow—begins when we stop running from the discomfort and start questioning the core beliefs driving these behaviors.

John's Story

John, a 36-year-old successful IT specialist, built a reputation for his strong work ethic and perfectionistic tendencies. However, beneath his professional success lay a deep-seated core belief that he wasn't good enough and needed to continuously prove his worth through productivity and achievement. This belief drove him to take on more work than he could handle, working long hours, often skipping breaks, and feeling that any misstep or failure would confirm his internal sense of incompetence. The constant pressure resulted in burnout, stress, and a persistent sense of dissatisfaction with both his work and personal life.

In his personal life, John found it difficult to connect emotionally with others. He often turned to distractions like binge-watching TV series, endlessly scrolling through his phone, and indulging in comfort food or alcohol when stressed. These quick fixes offered short-term relief but further distanced him from his emotions and the people around him. His romantic relationships suffered, as partners perceived him as emotionally distant and detached, making it hard for him to form deep, meaningful connections. His friends also noticed that he seemed absent during conversations, preoccupied with the need to stay busy or distracted.

In an effort to manage his feelings of inadequacy and relentless pressure to succeed, John increasingly turned to self-medicating behaviors that masked his emotional distress. After long, exhausting workdays, he often numbed himself with several drinks, convincing himself it was just a way to "unwind," though it frequently led to restless nights and groggy mornings. On weekends, he binged on junk food while mindlessly scrolling through social media, using the constant stimulation to drown out the nagging sense of emptiness and failure lurking beneath the surface. What started as occasional coping mechanisms gradually became habitual, leaving John caught in a cycle where temporary relief only deepened his disconnection from his emotions and the people around him.

The root of John's core belief lay in his upbringing. He grew up in a household where his parents were emotionally unavailable, often preoccupied with their own struggles. His father, a workaholic, frequently emphasized the importance of hard work and achievement as measures of success, while his mother, overwhelmed with her own emotional burdens, wasn't able to provide consistent validation or emotional support. As a result, John learned early on that his value came from what he could accomplish, rather than who he was as a person.

This lack of emotional support left John feeling unworthy and unseen. To cope, he adopted the belief that he needed to constantly prove himself through achievement, productivity, and busyness. He developed a habit of avoiding his feelings of inadequacy and loneliness by staying busy—whether at work or by distracting himself with food, alcohol, or technology. Each time John reached for these distractions, he reinforced the core belief that he wasn't enough and that avoiding his feelings was easier than confronting them.

These avoidance behaviors manifested in John's life as chronic stress, anxiety, and emotional disconnection. He experienced constant tension at work and felt isolated in his personal life, where his relationships remained shallow and unsatisfying. The belief that he wasn't good enough had embedded itself so deeply that John struggled to address it head-on, despite knowing that his distractions weren't helping him.

John's story highlights how negative core beliefs, tied to early life experiences, can lead to self-sabotaging behaviors like numbing through distractions. By turning to quick fixes like food, alcohol, or screen time, he avoided dealing with his emotions and reinforced his underlying belief of inadequacy. The cycle of avoidance left him disconnected from his true self and from others, perpetuating feelings of loneliness and dissatisfaction.

Through our work together, John began to explore the connection between his core belief and his behavior patterns. He learned that his worth was not tied to his productivity and that avoiding his uncomfortable feelings only magnified them over time. By addressing the root cause of his belief and learning to sit with discomfort rather than numb it, John began to break the cycle of avoidance and worked toward living more authentically.

Unrealistic Expectations of Self & Others

Some core beliefs lead us to set unrealistic expectations for ourselves and others, which sets us up for disappointment. We feel like we always need to do more, achieve more, and be more, leaving little room for self-care, compassion, or patience. This constant chase for perfection makes it difficult to appreciate our accomplishments, as we are always focused on what we haven't done, leading to a persistent sense of falling short. This can result in self-criticism, self-doubt, and a hesitation to try new things or take risks that could help us grow.

A lot of this pressure comes from a deep need for external validation and a fear of disappointing others. Instead of appreciating what we've already achieved or practicing gratitude, we get caught up in what we believe we need to do to be "good enough." This creates a moving target—no matter how much we do, it never feels like it's enough. When our high expectations inevitably aren't met, we feel frustrated and guilty, reinforcing the belief that we're somehow inadequate.

These unrealistic expectations don't just affect how we treat ourselves—they extend to our interactions with others. We project our fears of judgment onto them, assuming they expect as much from us as we expect from ourselves. This makes it difficult to ask for help because we feel we must prove our worth by doing everything independently. When we tie our identity and self-worth to meeting these impossible standards, the pressure builds. We start to feel like failures when we can't provide for our families or live up to perceived expectations.

Using "should" statements—like *I should be more successful* or *I should always be able to handle everything* - only compounds the issue. Constantly feeling like we're not measuring up wears down our sense of self-worth. By challenging these core beliefs and shifting our focus toward self-compassion and gratitude, rather than external validation, we can begin to develop a healthier, more fulfilling sense of self. Letting go of unrealistic expectations frees us to appreciate who we are and what we have, reducing stress and helping us live more authentically.

Imposter Syndrome

Imposter syndrome is incredibly common, affecting over 70% of people in the US at least once in their lives, especially high achievers. It's the internal experience of feeling like a fraud despite clear evidence of success, often accompanied by anxiety, depression, or constant self-doubt. Those who experience imposter syndrome struggle to internalize their accomplishments, feeling inadequate and fearing they'll be "found out." This can often be traced back to core beliefs formed early in life, where achievement and approval were closely tied to self-worth. For instance, growing up in a family that alternated between praise and criticism or placed immense importance on success can instill the belief that worth is based solely on accomplishments, leading to a perpetual fear of being exposed as a fraud.

Imposter Syndrome is often rooted in a mix of early influences, starting with family dynamics. Whether your upbringing was openly chaotic—marked by challenges like abuse or addiction—or seemed picture-perfect, your early experiences likely played a role. Families that valued achievement above all else or sent mixed signals—celebrating success one moment and criticizing failure the next—can quietly plant the seeds of self-doubt. Maybe you were labeled "the smart one" or "the overachiever," tying your self-worth to how effortlessly you performed or how hard you hustled. Even a nurturing family environment can leave its mark if you later find yourself in professions, like the arts, where critique is constant, and external validation feels rare and fleeting.

Social conditioning and biology don't help, either. In individualistic cultures like the U.S., success and self-worth are often interchangeable—especially for women taught to seek approval by being "perfect" or "pleasing." This pressure fuels perfectionism and a fear of failure, encouraging you to avoid risks and overcompensate with anxiety or endless preparation. Add in biology—like a heightened sensitivity to criticism and stronger emotional memory—and it's easy to see how negative feedback sticks, leading to endless rumination and self-comparison. Layer societal expectations and microaggressions on top, and you've got the perfect storm for feeling like you're never enough, no matter how much you achieve.

Women, in particular, are more susceptible to imposter syndrome due to long-standing gender stereotypes and societal expectations. From a young age, girls are often praised for being "good" and avoiding mistakes, which can cultivate perfectionism and a fear of failure. As they grow older, this pressure blurs the lines between approval, love, and self-worth, creating the belief that their value is tied to their achievements.

The emotional balancing act of juggling multiple roles, like excelling at work while managing family life, can further heighten feelings of inadequacy, as women feel they must be flawless in all areas to be perceived as competent.

Overcoming Imposter Syndrome starts with understanding its four main components: anxiety, perfectionism, self-doubt, and fear of failure. Anxiety often keeps you stuck in overthinking and worrying about outcomes you can't control, while perfectionism sets an impossible standard that leaves no room for mistakes or growth. Self-doubt whispers that you're not capable, no matter how much you've achieved, and fear of failure convinces you that taking risks isn't worth it. These feelings are fueled by negative self-talk—the relentless inner critic that highlights your flaws and dismisses your strengths.

Overly Critical of Self & Others

Core beliefs profoundly shape how we see ourselves and others. If you grew up in a household where you felt love and approval were conditional—tied to meeting unrealistic expectations or being perfect—you might have internalized the belief that you're only worthy if you're flawless. This belief fuels a harsh inner critic, always pushing you to meet impossible standards, leaving you feeling like you're never enough. Over time, this self-criticism can become second nature, deeply impacting your sense of self-worth and making it difficult to accept yourself as you are.

These ingrained beliefs don't just affect how you view yourself—they also influence how you see others. If you believe that your own needs or feelings are unimportant or invalid, you might project similar expectations onto the people around you, becoming overly critical when they don't meet the same high standards you impose on yourself. This tendency to judge others harshly can strain relationships, as you hold them to the same impossible standards you feel trapped by. It also makes it hard to empathize with others' imperfections, as their flaws can trigger reminders of your own deeply held insecurities.

In a household marked by narcissism or emotional neglect, you may have learned that your worth depends on how well you can please others or avoid conflict. This belief drives a constant need for external validation and a fear of rejection, leading to a vicious cycle of perfectionism and self-criticism. Seeking approval becomes the core way to feel valued, and any mistake or perceived failure can trigger harsh self-judgment. Over time, this reinforces the belief that you're inherently flawed, eroding your self-esteem and creating a hypercritical outlook on life.

This cycle doesn't just damage your self-worth—it also affects how you interact with others. Often, the same self-criticism that drives you can spill over into your relationships, leading to critical or judgmental behavior as a way to protect yourself from being criticized in return. You might feel compelled to point out others' flaws before they can notice yours, perpetuating a cycle of disconnection and dissatisfaction in your relationships.

These core beliefs become so deeply ingrained that they can dominate your life, making it feel almost impossible to break free from dysfunctional patterns. You might find yourself repeating negative behaviors in relationships or doubting your worthiness for love, success, or happiness. The fear of showing your true self, worried that you'll be rejected, can leave you in a constant state of anxiety and self-doubt. This, in turn, strengthens the cycle of self-criticism and judgment, both of yourself and others.

Breaking this cycle begins with recognizing that these beliefs are distorted perceptions from your past, not reflections of reality. By working to challenge these beliefs and adopting a more compassionate and realistic view of yourself, you can gradually shift away from self-criticism and judgment. This journey isn't easy, but by cultivating self-acceptance and empathy, you can begin to create healthier, more balanced relationships—with yourself and with others.

Olivia's Story

Olivia, a 39-year-old architect, built a successful career by maintaining high standards and an unwavering commitment to excellence. However, behind her professional achievements lay a relentless inner critic that drove her to constantly scrutinize her own performance and that of others. Whether at work or in her personal life, Olivia found it difficult to be satisfied with anything less than perfection, a mindset that strained her relationships and left her feeling isolated and unfulfilled.

Olivia's critical nature could be traced back to her upbringing in a household where love and approval were conditional. Her father, a high-achieving businessman, and her mother, who frequently withheld affection when Olivia didn't meet her expectations, instilled in her the belief that she was only worthy of love and acceptance if she was flawless. From a young age, Olivia learned to equate her self-worth with her ability to perform without error, internalizing a core belief that anything less than perfection was unacceptable.

As Olivia grew older, this belief manifested as a harsh inner critic that constantly pushed her to meet impossible standards. No matter how well she performed at work or how much she achieved, Olivia never felt good enough. She obsessed over minor mistakes, replaying them in her mind and criticizing herself for not being better. This self-criticism became a deeply ingrained part of her identity, affecting her sense of self-worth and making it difficult for her to accept herself as she was. The belief that she needed to be perfect to be worthy of love and success became a driving force in her life, leading to chronic stress and a pervasive sense of inadequacy.

Olivia's critical tendencies extended beyond herself, shaping how she viewed and interacted with others. She often projected her unrealistic expectations onto her colleagues and loved ones, becoming frustrated and judgmental when they failed to meet her high standards. In her relationships, Olivia struggled to empathize with others' imperfections, as they reminded her of her own perceived flaws. This lack of empathy created distance between her and those around her, as people found it difficult to connect with someone who seemed unable to accept them for who they were. Olivia's tendency to judge harshly not only alienated others but also reinforced her belief that she needed to be perfect to be accepted.

Recognizing the impact of her core beliefs on her life was a crucial step in Olivia's path toward self-compassion and personal growth. Through our work together, Olivia began to challenge the distorted perceptions she had developed in childhood, learning to see herself and others through a more compassionate and realistic lens. She worked on quieting her inner critic and understanding that mistakes and imperfections were a natural part of life and did not diminish her worth. As she developed a more balanced view of herself, Olivia also learned to be less judgmental of others, fostering more meaningful and empathetic relationships.

CHAPTER 8

Belief Cluster - Competency

Core Beliefs:

- "No matter what I do, or how hard I try, it's never enough"
- "I'm a failure and incapable"
- "I should have done better/more"

Self-Sabotaging Behaviors:

- **Difficulty asking for help** - Reluctance to seek assistance, driven by the belief that true competence requires self-reliance and that asking for help signals inadequacy or failure.

- **Overworking/burnout** – A desire to prove competency through excessive work, often leading to burnout.

- **Procrastination** – The act of delaying or avoiding tasks, often by focusing on less important activities, despite knowing it may lead to negative consequences.

Difficulty Asking for Help

Not asking for help is one of the sneakiest forms of self-sabotage, and it often ties back to our core beliefs about competence and worthiness. Many of us have picked up the idea that asking for help somehow makes us inadequate or weak. We convince ourselves that we should be able to handle everything on our own, and if we can't, it must mean there's something wrong with us. The fear of being "found out" or exposed as incompetent makes us struggle in silence—even when asking for help could be a game changer. Ironically, by not asking for support, we make things harder for ourselves and strengthen the very beliefs we're trying to avoid.

At the core of this behavior is the fear of judgment or rejection. We worry that if we ask for help, others will see us as a burden, or worse, they'll think less of us. The thought of being judged or feeling embarrassed is so uncomfortable that we'd rather push through on our own, even when we're drowning. We tell ourselves it's better to struggle alone than risk looking needy or incapable. But in isolating ourselves, we end up feeding the belief that we're on our own in the world, which only adds to the loneliness and reinforces the idea that we can't rely on anyone else.

And then there's the guilt or shame that often comes with asking for help. Some people feel like they're inconveniencing others, or they believe that needing help means they're failing at being self-sufficient. It's that little voice whispering, "You should be able to do this yourself." This guilt can keep us from reaching out, even when the people around us would be more than happy to support us.

The irony is that by not asking for help, we often create the exact outcomes we're afraid of. Taking on too much and refusing to reach out can lead to burnout, missed deadlines, or making mistakes. And what does that do? It makes us feel incompetent, reinforcing the very core belief we were trying to avoid in the first place. In the end, this only strengthens the feeling that we're unsupported and have to navigate life solo, further cutting us off from the help and connection we actually need. Over time, this pattern becomes a self-sabotage loop.

Here's the reality: asking for help isn't a sign of weakness or failure. It's simply recognizing that we're human and have limits, just like everyone else. When we challenge these harmful core beliefs and shift our mindset, we open ourselves up to connection and support. Learning to ask for help—whether it's from friends, family, or coworkers—lets us share the load and create opportunities for connection and reciprocity. The fear of being "found out" or judged often fades when we realize that everyone struggles, and asking for help doesn't make us less capable. In fact, it's part of what makes us stronger.

Macy's Story

Macy, a 38-year-old mother of three young children, lived with the core belief that she had to handle everything on her own to be a "good" and competent mother. Known for her ability to juggle the demands of parenting, maintaining the household, and working part-time, Macy constantly pushed herself to manage everything without asking for help. She believed that needing assistance would mean she was failing as a mother and not living up to her own high standards of self-sufficiency. As a result, she struggled with exhaustion, stress, and an overwhelming sense of inadequacy.

In her personal life, Macy rarely reached out for support, even when she felt overwhelmed. She worried that asking for help would make her seem incapable in the eyes of her family, friends, and even her husband. This fear of being judged as "not good enough" kept her silent, leading her to handle all the household tasks, childcare responsibilities, and even her part-time job on her own. Her husband had offered to help numerous times, but Macy insisted on doing everything herself, feeling guilty at the mere thought of delegating tasks. One evening stood out vividly in her memory—she was up past midnight, frantically frosting cupcakes for her daughter's school event while folding laundry and answering work emails. When her husband gently suggested he could take over the cupcakes, Macy snapped, insisting she was "fine," even though she was on the verge of tears. She spent the next day exhausted and irritable, resenting her husband for not "seeing how much she did," despite refusing his help.

The root of Macy's core belief lay in her upbringing. Growing up, Macy watched her mother take on a similar role—managing the household with little to no help, despite working full-time. Macy's mother often told her that a "strong woman" took care of everything herself, and this message was reinforced by Macy's father, who rarely helped around the house. Macy internalized the belief that being a good mother and wife meant being self-sufficient, handling everything on her own, and not burdening others with her struggles.

This lack of support and the belief that strength meant doing everything alone left Macy feeling overwhelmed and isolated. To cope, she adopted the habit of overextending herself and silently carrying the weight of all her obligations. Each time she felt exhausted but refused to ask for help, it reinforced her fear that needing assistance meant she was failing, further embedding the belief that she had to do everything herself. She often found herself resentful and emotionally distant from her family, feeling unappreciated even though she never communicated her needs.

These avoidant behaviors manifested in Macy's life as chronic stress, burnout, and emotional distance from her family. She experienced constant tension at home and felt isolated in her personal life, where her relationships remained distant and unfulfilling. The belief that she had to do it all alone embedded itself so deeply that Macy struggled to ask for support, despite knowing it could help.

Macy's story highlights how her core belief about being self-sufficient, which was tied to her early life experiences, led to self-sabotaging behaviors like refusing to ask for help. By trying to maintain control over everything herself, Macy avoided dealing with her feelings of inadequacy, which reinforced her underlying belief that she was failing if she needed assistance. The cycle of avoidance left her disconnected from her true self and from others, perpetuating feelings of exhaustion, stress, and emotional isolation.

Through therapy, we began to explore the connection between Macy's core belief and her behavior patterns. She learned that her worth was not tied to her ability to handle everything alone, and that asking for help didn't make her any less capable. We practiced small steps, like allowing her husband to handle bedtime routines without stepping in to "fix" things, even if it wasn't done her way. By addressing the root cause of her belief and learning to lean on others, Macy began to break the cycle of self-sabotage. Over time, she discovered that accepting support not only lightened her load but also deepened her connection with her family, helping her feel more present, appreciated, and less alone.

Overworking & Burnout

Core beliefs can easily push us toward burnout and overworking, especially when we tie our self-worth to how much we achieve. This mindset often leads us to prioritize work and accomplishments over everything else, neglecting self-care, boundaries, and the need for rest. We convince ourselves that we always need to be doing more, never giving ourselves permission to slow down. Some of this comes from our hustle culture.

This constant drive also comes from a deep fear of failure and a craving for external validation. We believe that to be respected and valued, we must consistently meet or exceed expectations. This fear leads to overcommitting and overextending ourselves, with the belief that taking a break or slowing down will be seen as weakness. But this mindset is a fast track to burnout, leaving no space for rest or balance in our lives.

These beliefs also make it hard to set healthy boundaries. We might struggle to say no to extra responsibilities, fearing disappointment or the appearance of incompetence. Without clear boundaries, we take on too much, sacrificing personal time and the activities that help us relax and recharge. When work consumes our entire life, it becomes nearly impossible to disconnect or find relief from stress.

Neglecting self-care and skipping breaks only adds fuel to the fire. Skipping meals, losing sleep, and ignoring signs that we need to slow down all lead to serious health consequences and a persistent feeling of being overwhelmed. To escape this cycle, we need to challenge the belief that our worth is defined by productivity. Embracing self-care, setting boundaries, and making time for breaks not only prevents burnout but also helps us find a healthier, more sustainable balance in life. In turn, this actually makes us more efficient with our work, which makes us more productive, so it's a win-win.

Procrastination

Procrastination is often a coping mechanism for feeling overwhelmed, but instead of resolving anything, it hinders productivity and stops you from addressing the root cause of your stress. It's frequently blamed on poor time management, but at its core, procrastination is more about avoiding uncomfortable emotions. When we're anxious about not meeting expectations—whether our own or others'—we tend to put things off. It's not because we lack time, but because the task stirs up anxiety or fear of failure. Delaying it provides temporary relief from those uncomfortable feelings.

This behavior is deeply connected to our core beliefs. If you believe you need to be perfect to be valued, any task that might expose imperfections becomes a significant source of stress. The fear of not being "good enough" can lead to procrastination as a way to dodge potential failure. By putting things off, you avoid facing this fear in the short term, but it reinforces the belief that you're only worthy if everything you do is flawless.

We also procrastinate to escape the discomfort certain tasks bring. Whether it's boredom, frustration, or the difficulty of the work itself, these negative emotions drive us to delay. Our brains are wired to avoid pain and seek pleasure, so we shy away from tasks that feel unpleasant. This avoidance can also stem from the belief that we're lazy or not capable. If you've internalized the idea that you're inherently lazy or incompetent, procrastinating can become a way to avoid confronting those painful thoughts about yourself.

Recognizing procrastination as emotional avoidance, rather than a time management issue, helps us address the root problem. By challenging core beliefs and cultivating self-compassion, we can reduce the emotional burden of tasks and change the habit. Shifting our perspective to see mistakes and imperfections as part of the learning experience makes it easier to face tasks head-on and manage our time more effectively.

Stephanie's Story

Stephanie, a 35-year-old computer sciences professor, often found herself paralyzed when it came to writing and submitting research papers, despite knowing their significance to her academic career. Her procrastination had become a recurring theme, causing missed opportunities for publication and collaboration. While she was highly respected in her field and possessed a wealth of knowledge, Stephanie constantly struggled with the anxiety that accompanied the process of drafting, revising, and submitting her work. Instead of starting early, she tended to put off writing until the submission deadline loomed uncomfortably close, leaving her scrambling to finish and feeling unsatisfied with the end result.

Stephanie's struggles with procrastination stemmed from her childhood, where she was raised in a household that placed immense pressure on achieving excellence. Her mother, in particular, set high standards and often emphasized success and status. Praise was reserved for flawless accomplishments, and any minor mistakes were met with criticism. Stephanie vividly recalled competing in a middle school tennis tournament, where she finished in second place. Instead of celebrating her achievement, her mother's first words were, "Why didn't you win first?" This formative experience reinforced a deep-seated belief that anything less than perfect was a failure.

As an adult, this belief manifested in Stephanie's approach to writing research papers. She felt an overwhelming need to produce groundbreaking work that would be featured in the most prestigious journals, fearing that anything less would expose her shortcomings. This pressure to achieve perfection created immense anxiety, leading her to avoid the writing process altogether. Procrastination provided her with temporary relief from the fear of judgment and inadequacy. However, the avoidance only fueled her internal narrative that she must be flawless to be worthy, perpetuating a cycle of stress and self-doubt.

Stephanie's procrastination was further reinforced by her aversion to the emotional discomfort that writing evoked. The uncertainty of research findings, the possibility of peer criticism, and the complexity of articulating her ideas with precision all triggered feelings of self-doubt. She feared that her work might not meet the rigorous standards of her field or, worse, might reveal that she was not as competent as others perceived her to be. To protect herself from these emotions, she delayed starting until the last possible moment, when the pressure to complete the work outweighed the fear of imperfection.

Stephanie gradually began to recognize the emotional roots of her procrastination. Understanding that her avoidance was linked to her deep-seated belief about competency and self-worth, she started challenging these thoughts. She worked on shifting her mindset by reminding herself that academic writing was an iterative process, not an immediate measure of her value. Stephanie also began practicing self-compassion, allowing herself to make mistakes during the drafting phase without self-judgment. Over time, she found that breaking tasks into smaller, manageable steps helped her build momentum and reduce the emotional weight she once attached to writing. As she continued to challenge her perfectionistic tendencies, she experienced a greater sense of accomplishment and confidence in her work.

CHAPTER 9

Belief Cluster - Vulnerability & Judgment

Core Beliefs:

- "I can't protect myself (emotionally)"
- "I'm a burden to others"
- "I can't trust my judgment"

Self-Sabotaging Behaviors:

- **Anger** – Often a defense mechanism for feeling vulnerable or judged.

- **Avoidance** – Avoiding situations where one might feel judged or exposed to vulnerability.

Anger

Anger is a common "go-to" emotion for those dealing with impactful experiences from childhood, but it usually masks something more vulnerable, like sadness, grief, or feelings of inadequacy. Think of anger like an iceberg: there's the 10% that's visible, but there's so much more beneath the surface.

Anger is often just the tip, with deeper emotions like hurt, shame, or fear hidden below. These underlying feelings can be harder to recognize or express, so anger becomes the default response because it's easier to show and feels less vulnerable. It keeps others at a distance and can feel empowering and energizing. A small comment from a loved one might trigger intense rage, or a minor mistake could lead to harsh self-criticism. Over time, this pent-up anger can build, leading to emotional outbursts that we later regret, trapping us in a cycle of shame, frustration, and self-blame.

Core beliefs play a powerful role in how we experience and manage anger, often steering us toward unhealthy reactions. Many people with anger issues carry the belief that feeling angry is inherently wrong or unacceptable. This leads to a cycle where the initial anger is followed by guilt or self-judgment, which only intensifies the emotion and makes it harder to handle. On the other hand, some people grew up in a household where anger was modeled for them, so it's the only way they know how to express emotion.

In some families, anger is more acceptable than other emotions. You might have learned that expressing anger is okay, but showing sadness, insecurity, or embarrassment is not. As a result, you use anger to mask those more vulnerable feelings. This protective strategy helps you avoid feeling exposed, but it also prevents you from addressing the real issues beneath your anger. Over time, this makes it more difficult to process the emotions driving your reactions.

Understanding anger is key to developing a healthier relationship with it. One of the biggest misconceptions is that anger is a purely negative emotion. In reality, anger often feels empowering because it's tied to a sense of righteousness or justice. When we feel wronged, anger can give us a sense of control or moral superiority. This can explain why we sometimes get stuck in behaviors that keep us angry, such as blaming others or fixating on perceived injustices, as these behaviors temporarily boost our self-esteem.

It's also important to differentiate between anger and aggression. Anger is an emotion—something we all feel—while aggression is a behavior, and it's something we can control. Many people waste energy trying to suppress their anger, thinking they can manage the emotion directly, but that approach usually backfires. It's far more productive to acknowledge and validate the emotion of anger while focusing on controlling the aggressive impulses that may follow. This allows you to manage anger in a way that's less destructive and more aligned with your true intentions.

Another crucial point is that venting your anger doesn't make it disappear; in fact, it can do the opposite. Venting often reinforces the emotion, keeping you stuck in a loop of frustration rather than addressing the real issues behind the anger. Instead of venting, try to recognize and acknowledge your anger while identifying the more vulnerable emotions underneath.

Your anger triggers—whether it's a specific person, situation, or even a small comment—can offer clues about what's really going on beneath the surface. For example, if you find yourself getting angry when you feel ignored, it may be because deep down, you're feeling lonely or unimportant. Different emotions can fuel your anger at different times, or even all at once. Understanding what's truly driving your anger is the first step in managing it more effectively.

That said, sometimes anger is simply anger—it's a natural, human emotion, and it's okay to feel it. But by digging deeper into what's behind your anger, you may discover that it's often linked to your core beliefs. Recognizing and addressing the underlying emotions can help you manage your anger in a healthier, more balanced way, rather than letting it control your actions or damage your relationships.

Eli's Story

Eli, a 45-year-old construction foreman, was known for his quick temper and explosive reactions, both on the job and at home. His coworkers respected him for his work ethic, but they also treaded carefully around him, aware that a minor mistake or offhand comment could set him off. At home, Eli's family often bore the brunt of his anger, which erupted over seemingly trivial issues. Despite his outward displays of anger, Eli felt a deep sense of shame and frustration after each outburst, trapped in a cycle of rage and regret that he struggled to understand or control.

One moment that stood out for Eli was an argument with his teenage son over something as simple as the dishes. After a long, stressful day at work, Eli came home to find the sink full despite having asked his son to clean up earlier. Without pausing to consider why the chore hadn't been done, Eli exploded—raising his voice, slamming a cabinet door, and accusing his son of being lazy and disrespectful. The intensity of his reaction far outweighed the situation, leaving his son retreating to his room in silence. Minutes after the outburst, Eli felt the familiar wave of guilt wash over him. His anger wasn't truly about the dishes; it was the culmination of unspoken frustrations, stress, and an underlying fear that he was failing as a father—the very thing he was trying to avoid.

The roots of Eli's anger could be traced back to his childhood, where he grew up in a household filled with emotional turbulence. His father, a strict and emotionally distant man, often expressed his frustrations through anger, while his mother, who was more nurturing, struggled to protect Eli and his siblings from their father's wrath. As a child, Eli learned to associate anger with power and control, and he subconsciously adopted it as a defense mechanism to cope with the emotional chaos around him. Beneath this anger, however, was a deep-seated grief—a grief for the loss of a carefree childhood, for the lack of a safe and loving environment, and for the missed opportunities to develop a positive sense of self-worth.

As Eli entered adulthood, this unresolved grief began to manifest in his closest relationships. The anger he had adopted as a coping mechanism now flared up in response to situations that triggered his underlying feelings of inadequacy and loss. A seemingly innocuous remark from his wife about work could provoke an intense reaction, not because of the comment itself, but because it tapped into his deep-seated fear of not being good enough. Similarly, a minor mistake at work would lead to harsh self-criticism, rooted in the core belief that any failure was a reflection of his worthlessness. These bursts of anger were less about the immediate circumstances and more about the unaddressed grief and sadness simmering beneath the surface.

Eli's struggle with anger was compounded by his belief that feeling and expressing anger was inherently wrong, a belief instilled in him by his father's rigid expectations. This belief created a cycle where the anger he felt was quickly followed by self-judgment and guilt, intensifying the emotion rather than diffusing it. In other moments, Eli clung to the notion that venting his anger was necessary to prevent it from building up, leading him to ruminate on perceived wrongs and magnify his sense of injustice. This approach only served to reinforce his anger, keeping him locked in a pattern of destructive behavior that harmed both his relationships and his self-esteem.

Recognizing that his anger was a mask for deeper emotions was a pivotal moment for Eli. Through our work together, he began to explore the grief, sadness, and fear that underpinned his rage. He learned that anger, while natural, was often the visible tip of an iceberg of more vulnerable emotions. By acknowledging and addressing these underlying feelings, Eli started to break the vicious cycle of anger and self-judgment that had dominated his life. He worked on separating his anger from aggressive behaviors, allowing himself to feel the emotion without letting it control his actions. This shift in perspective enabled Eli to manage his anger in a healthier way, improving his relationships and helping him reconnect with the parts of himself that he had long buried under layers of unresolved grief.

Avoidance

As children, when things became too intense, we might have "checked out" by daydreaming, spending a lot of time alone, or escaping into our own little world. These habits were survival mechanisms—they helped us cope when things felt out of control. But as we grow older, these same patterns can become ingrained ways of dealing with stress and emotions that no longer serve us.

As adults, these early coping mechanisms can show up as procrastination, busyness, laziness, staying in our comfort zones, having difficulty being alone with our thoughts, various numbing behaviors, etc. When something stirs up strong emotions, we might avoid it altogether because it feels too overwhelming to confront. If we've internalized the belief that our feelings don't matter, or that we must stay in control at all costs, we tend to steer clear of situations that bring up uncomfortable emotions. While this helps us avoid pain in the short term, it also leads to missed opportunities in our personal & professional growth and relationships.

Avoidance doesn't just affect how we handle stress—it also influences how we manage vulnerability in relationships. Instead of dealing with difficult emotions or opening up to others, we might distract ourselves or numb the feelings to keep them at bay. Overworking can become a way to avoid facing deeper issues, while turning to food or alcohol may dull the emotional pain. However, these behaviors create a cycle where vulnerability is continually avoided, leading to a growing sense of disconnection from both ourselves and the people we care about.

At the core of these avoidant behaviors is the belief that facing emotions is too painful, too risky. We come to believe that if we open ourselves up to those feelings, we'll lose control or be overwhelmed. Breaking this cycle means challenging these core beliefs and learning to tolerate discomfort in healthier ways. It's about gradually allowing ourselves to feel vulnerable, to sit with emotions as they come, rather than pushing them away. In doing so, we can reconnect with our true selves and build more meaningful, fulfilling relationships—both with others and with ourselves.

Discovery Prompt:
Identifying the Roots of Self-Sabotage

This exercise will help you identify self-sabotaging behaviors rooted in negative core beliefs, the emotions that accompany them, and their origins. After reviewing the example, set aside 5-10 minutes to work through the following steps:

1. **Spot a self-sabotaging behavior:** Think about a pattern or habit that's been getting in the way of your goals or keeping you from living in alignment with your values. It could be procrastination, avoiding conflict, isolating yourself, overcommitting, or neglecting self-care. Pick one that stands out and write it down.

2. **Ask yourself, "What belief is behind this?":** What negative core belief might be fueling this behavior? Is it the one you identified in Chapter 2? Is it a new one? Check the list below if you need some ideas, then write down the belief that resonates the most:

   • "I'm powerless"
   • "I'm unworthy"
   • "I'm a disappointment"
   • "Nobody respects me"
   • "I'm not good enough/smart enough"
   • "I'm a failure"
   • "I'm responsible for other people's feelings"
   • "Love is conditional"

3. **Name the primary emotion:** What emotion is wrapped up in this belief and behavior? It could be

shame, guilt, fear, anxiety, or disappointment. Write down what comes up for you.

4. **Think back to when you first remember feeling this way**: Recall an early memory when you experienced this same emotion or belief. What happened? Write down the situation and how it made you feel. There may be one that sticks out, or there may be several.

5. **Connect the dots**: Review your answers and reflect on how these core beliefs and emotions are tied to your self-sabotaging behavior today.

Example:

Self-sabotaging behavior: "I have such a hard time saying 'no.' I constantly overcommit to helping others and neglect my own needs, even when I'm exhausted."

Core belief: "I'm responsible for other people's emotions and I don't want to disappoint anyone" or "Love is conditional (it's based on what I do, not who I am)."

Primary emotion: "I feel guilt and fear—if I don't help, I'll feel worthless and be perceived as being selfish."

Earliest memory: "When I was 10, my dad lost his job and was going through a tough time. He'd say, 'I'm so grateful you're here—you're the only one I can rely on.' I felt proud but also terrified that if I stopped helping, I'd let him down and he wouldn't be okay on his own."

Reflection: "I realize now that my overcommitting is tied to the belief that I have to take care of others to be valuable. This belief, driven by a fear of not being good enough, leads me to sacrifice my own well-being."

By connecting your self-sabotaging behaviors to the core beliefs and emotions driving them, you'll gain clarity on why these patterns persist. This awareness is the first step toward creating healthier habits and treating yourself with more compassion.

PART 3

MAKING CHANGES

CHAPTER 10

We All Have Parts

Imagine you're driving a bus, and all the different parts of you—like characters with their own personalities, feelings, and agendas—are on board. Some parts are loud, jumping up to grab the wheel, while others hang out quietly in the back, just observing. Each one has its own way of trying to help or protect you, even if it doesn't always feel like it.

Up at the front, there's that frantic, anxiety-ridden part, white-knuckling the wheel, eyes darting for danger, and shouting orders like the fate of the world depends on it staying in control. Riding shotgun is the ruthless perfectionist, a relentless backseat driver obsessing over every rule, every speed limit, and every minor misstep. And let's not forget the ever-apologetic people-pleaser, scrambling to keep everyone else on the bus happy—even if it means veering off-course to make snack runs you never agreed to. These parts don't just grab the wheel—they hijack it, recklessly steering you down paths you never intended to take.

Then there are the quieter parts sitting in the back. These might be the parts carrying old pain or sadness—the ones that feel too wounded or afraid to speak up. Maybe they've been told to stay hidden for so long that they've stopped trying to drive at all. But even when they're not fighting for the front seat, you still feel their presence. They can shift the mood of the whole bus or stir up the other parts.

Your true Self? That's the calm, confident driver who's supposed to be steering. When you're in touch with your Self, you can let each part of you have its say, but you stay in control of the wheel. The goal isn't to push these parts away or ignore them. It's to listen to them, understand why they're there, and help them feel heard so they can relax and trust you to drive. When that happens, all your parts can ride along in harmony, and you can steer the bus to the destination that truly feels right.

Meet Your Parts

Internal Family Systems (IFS) is an approach developed by psychologist Richard Schwartz back in the 1980s, and over time it's become incredibly popular for helping people understand the different parts of their minds and how those parts interact. Think of it like the way your body has different organs, each doing its part to keep you alive. In the same way, your mind has different parts, and each part has its own role. IFS looks at these parts like a family, where each member has a job to do, even if they don't always get along.

In IFS, the main parts are divided into Protectors and Exiles. The Protectors are split into two groups: Managers and Firefighters. Their job? To keep the Exiles—those parts of us that feel unsafe, rejected, or hurt—hidden or under control. These Exiles are usually formed when we experience emotions or situations we weren't able to process, often starting in childhood. In pop psychology, you've probably heard this referred to as your "inner child." These exiled parts carry a heavy burden—core beliefs that need to be addressed so they can stop living in the shadows. The Protectors—like Managers and Firefighters—step in to keep those painful feelings in check, preventing them from messing with our day-to-day lives.

Let's be clear: *parts are NOT personality traits.* They're pieces of a larger system designed to help you survive. The problem is that this system was often formed when you were younger, so it's outdated. It's like using a flip phone in a world of smartphones. Protectors might fear that if you heal or change those old operating systems, they'll lose their job or purpose. They worry they'll be left behind or won't know what to do. But the truth is, these parts can still help you in new, healthier ways once healing takes place, and their protective roles evolve.

Example: Sarah

Sarah grew up in a family where showing nervousness or worry wasn't an option. Whenever she felt anxious as a kid, especially in social settings, her parents would tell her to "toughen up" and stop being so sensitive. Over time, this created an Exile—Sarah's anxious part, the one that got nervous in social situations but was never allowed to express it.

To protect this anxious Exile, Sarah's Manager developed a strategy: avoid social situations or spend hours preparing to look calm and confident. Her Manager kept the anxiety hidden by making sure she was always busy with work or study, so she'd never appear rattled.

But when the pressure built up and the Manager couldn't keep things under control, Sarah's Firefighter would step in. The Firefighter's job was to put out the emotional fire quickly, even if it wasn't the healthiest way. For Sarah, that looked like canceling plans at the last minute or downing a drink before a social event to calm her nerves. These actions kept the anxiety at bay for a while, but afterward, they left her feeling guilty and even more isolated.

Example: John

John grew up in a family where success was the only option, and showing fear or weakness was out of the question. His parents expected him to excel at everything, and any sign of anxiety or failure was met with criticism. This created an Exile—John's anxious part that constantly worried he wasn't good enough.

John's Manager learned to protect that Exile by making him work harder than everyone else, avoiding failure at all costs. His Manager kept him hyper-organized and laser-focused on his job to keep the anxiety from surfacing. But this also turned John into a perfectionist—always over-preparing for meetings and tasks to hide his fear of failure.

But when the workload became too much or John faced a huge challenge, the Manager couldn't keep the anxiety in check. That's when his Firefighter took over. To avoid feeling the panic of not being good enough, John would procrastinate, suddenly finding himself scrolling through social media or binge-watching TV instead of working. Sure, this numbed the fear for a bit, but it also led to last-minute stress, causing more anxiety about deadlines and performance.

The Protectors—Managers and Firefighters—do their best to keep things balanced by managing or hiding the anxious Exiles. When one type of Protector can't keep things in check, the other steps in, even if their methods cause more issues in the long run. Whether it's avoiding social situations or drowning in distractions, these parts are trying to protect you in their own way, even if it doesn't always seem helpful. It's important to remember there are no bad parts, and all parts have good intentions, they just need a software update. The key is understanding these parts so they can work together in a healthier way, allowing you to cope with your emotions and navigate life more smoothly.

Protectors: Managers

Manager parts are like the overworked, stressed-out employees in your mind who are trying to keep your life running smoothly. They're the parts of you that constantly stay ahead of problems, making sure everything is in control so you can feel safe and functional. These parts handle the day-to-day operations—keeping you productive, avoiding conflict, and making sure things don't fall apart. While they mean well, they often end up completely exhausted from trying to manage every little detail of your life.

These manager parts can show up in a lot of different ways. Maybe you have a perfectionist part that's always pushing you to do everything flawlessly, terrified of making mistakes or being criticized. Or maybe you have a people-pleaser part that avoids conflict at all costs, always bending over backward to make sure everyone else is happy—even when it means neglecting your own needs. Then there's the fixer—the part that thinks it's your job to solve everyone else's problems—or the overthinker, who analyzes every situation to death just to avoid any surprises. These parts are constantly clocked in, trying to prevent anything from going wrong.

Other manager parts are the planners and organizers. They're the ones obsessing over every detail of a project, making sure you're always prepared. That part of you that's double-checking everything and always planning for the worst-case scenario? That's a manager hard at work. These parts truly believe that if they can stay on top of everything, they can keep your world from falling apart—and stop any emotional pain from sneaking in.

But here's the catch: these manager parts often carry too much. They're so focused on controlling things and preventing problems that they end up leaving you drained. Their main goal is to protect you from feeling old wounds or emotions you've buried, but in doing so, they sometimes push too hard, leaving no room for you to breathe. When these parts feel heard and acknowledged for all the hard work they've been doing, they can start to relax a bit. They don't have to control everything—they just need to feel like they're doing enough to keep you safe. Once they trust that, they can step back, finding a healthier balance where they handle what's actually in their control without carrying the weight of the world.

Samantha's Story

Samantha had always been the one who held everything together—at least, that's what it felt like to her. Her days were a constant blur of to-do lists, double-checking schedules, and making sure everything ran smoothly. She knew the perfectionist part of her well, the one that wouldn't let her rest until everything was flawless, down to the smallest detail. Then there was the people-pleaser, who kept her smiling and agreeable, even when she wanted to scream. Every moment felt like a tightrope walk, balancing the needs of others with her relentless drive to avoid mistakes, conflict, or discomfort. It was exhausting.

Over time, the weight of these manager parts became overwhelming. Her overthinker wouldn't let her sleep, running endless loops of "what ifs" through her mind. The fixer part showed up uninvited in her friendships and relationships, stepping in to solve problems that weren't hers to solve. Samantha's manager parts believed they were protecting her from chaos, from the old wounds of failure and rejection, but instead, they left her drained and anxious. It wasn't until she began to understand these parts, giving them space to feel heard, that they began to relax their grip.

As Samantha continued exploring these parts of herself with me, she started to notice how deeply ingrained these patterns were. Her perfectionist part wasn't just about avoiding criticism; it was rooted in a childhood where mistakes were harshly critiqued, and love felt conditional on her achievements. The people-pleaser had been born out of years of trying to keep peace in a volatile home, where conflict often led to emotional withdrawal. As she listened to these parts, she began to understand their fears and the burdens they carried for so long. They weren't the enemy—they were just trying to protect her. Slowly, as she validated their efforts, she found that they didn't need to work so hard. The overthinker could rest when she realized that not every detail needed to be controlled, and the fixer could step back when she accepted that it wasn't her job to solve everyone else's problems. This newfound awareness allowed her to reclaim moments of peace, recognizing that she was enough, even when everything wasn't perfectly managed.

Protectors: Firefighters

Firefighters are the parts of us that rush in when emotional pain gets too intense to handle. When old wounds (Exiles) are triggered—stirring up feelings like shame, fear, or worthlessness—firefighters jump into action. Unlike managers, who try to keep us from feeling hurt in the first place, firefighters are reactive. They'll use whatever it takes to numb or distract us from the pain. This might look like binge eating, drinking, self-harm, panic attacks, or even dissociating. While these behaviors might seem extreme or harmful, their main goal is to protect us from emotions that feel too overwhelming to face.

Firefighters don't mess around. When they sense an emotional fire, they act fast. For example, after a tough day that stirs up old feelings of unworthiness, a firefighter might push someone to drink or overeat just to escape those emotions. It's not about causing harm—the firefighter part is trying to shield the person from the deep pain underneath. They're after instant relief, doing whatever it takes to stop the hurt, even if it's only temporary.

Firefighter behaviors can range from what society might see as "acceptable," like overworking or excessive exercising, to more destructive coping mechanisms like substance abuse or gambling. The key difference between firefighters and managers is how they operate. Managers work proactively, trying to control things to avoid emotional pain. Firefighters, on the other hand, react impulsively when things feel too hard to handle. For instance, a manager might rigidly control their diet to feel in control, while a firefighter might binge eat when the pressure gets too much. Both are trying to protect you from the same deep pain, but firefighters act in the heat of the moment, driven by the fear that the emotional pain will take over if they don't do something fast.

Firefighters are often misunderstood—and even hated—by both the person and those around them. It's easy to feel ashamed for turning to destructive coping mechanisms, which can lead to a vicious cycle of guilt and self-loathing. Firefighters carry beliefs like, "I know I'm defective, and I can't let anyone see that," or "I have to keep these emotions from taking over." They jump into action to keep these vulnerable feelings hidden, using whatever method they think will work.

Even though firefighter behaviors can be harmful, they serve a critical role in protecting us during emotional crises. They're like the first responders in our internal system, showing up when things get overwhelming. The goal in IFS isn't to get rid of these parts but to understand their good intentions and help them find healthier ways to protect us without causing harm.

Amelia's Story

Amelia had always been the one to find comfort in distraction. When the silence of her thoughts became too much, her nights turned into episodes of mindless eating or hours spent lost in TV shows. She knew the firefighter part of her well, the one that would swoop in when the feelings of unworthiness or shame started to creep in. Then there was the dissociative part, the one that could turn off her emotions like a switch when things felt too overwhelming. Every moment of quiet became a ticking clock, waiting for the pain to bubble up, and her firefighters always acted fast to avoid it. It was a cycle she couldn't seem to escape.

Over time, the weight of these reactive behaviors became exhausting. Her binge-eater wouldn't let her stop until she was numb, filling the void with food until the emotional fire was doused. The part of her that dissociated would zone out in conversations, checking out completely when the discomfort got too intense. Amelia's firefighters believed they were protecting her from the deep pain of her childhood, the wounds of feeling unworthy and unloved, but instead, they left her feeling ashamed and out of control. It wasn't until she began to understand these parts in therapy, giving them space to be heard, that she started to see what they were really trying to do.

As Amelia explored these parts of herself through Internal Family Systems (IFS), she began to uncover the patterns that had controlled her for so long. Her binge-eating wasn't just about avoiding emotional pain—it was rooted in the deep shame she had carried since childhood, when any sign of weakness was met with harsh criticism. The part of her that dissociated had learned early on that shutting down was the safest way to avoid emotional overwhelm, especially when her feelings were ignored or invalidated at home. As she began to listen to these parts, she realized that they were terrified of her being consumed by the very emotions they were trying to keep at bay. They weren't trying to hurt her—they were doing everything they could to protect her from drowning in those old wounds.

Slowly, as Amelia began to understand their fears and validate their efforts, she found that these parts didn't need to act so impulsively. The binge-eater could pause when she acknowledged the shame underneath, and the dissociative part could rest when she realized she didn't have to disappear in order to feel safe. This newfound awareness gave her the space to make different choices, to allow herself to feel her emotions without the panic of avoidance. It wasn't perfect, but with each step, Amelia reclaimed pieces of herself, learning that she could face her pain without being consumed by it. And in that process, she discovered a deeper sense of peace, knowing that she would be okay, even in moments of discomfort.

Exiles (aka Wounds or "Inner Child")

Exiles are the wounded parts of us—those younger, vulnerable versions that hold onto deep emotional pain from the past. They're stuck in time, clinging to hurt, painful memories, and beliefs that formed when something overwhelming happened. Maybe an exile feels unlovable, broken, or like they can't do anything right, all because of difficult experiences or relationships early on. These feelings get buried deep, but they don't disappear. Instead, they stay locked away, carrying the weight of shame, worthlessness, or fear, just waiting to be acknowledged and healed.

Your inner system works overtime to protect these exiled parts, usually by creating other parts that act like shields. These protectors might show up as perfectionism, avoidance, or even anger—anything that helps you avoid feeling the exile's raw pain. For example, someone who felt unworthy of love as a child might develop a part that constantly seeks approval, trying to dodge the old wound of rejection. These protective strategies can run our lives behind the scenes, all because those vulnerable parts are still hurting.

Healing begins when we start to offer love, compassion, and connection to these exiled parts. They need the care and understanding they didn't get back then. When we listen to their pain and give them the reassurance they've been needing, they can finally start to release the heavy burdens they've been carrying. For instance, if a part of you feels like you're "too much" because of things that happened in childhood, offering that part gentleness and acceptance can create a deep emotional release. That's the moment the exile feels heard and seen, and that can be extremely powerful.

These exiles don't just affect us internally—they also play a big role in our relationships. Often, we're drawn to people with similar wounds because something about it feels familiar. It's like we unconsciously hope they'll fix what's broken inside of us. For example, if both you and your partner struggle with feeling "not enough," you might choose each other, hoping the relationship will heal that wound. But the truth is, these exiled parts need healing from within, not from someone else.

Ultimately, these exiled parts are desperate to be understood and to release the pain they've carried for so long. They hold onto those negative core beliefs, like being unlovable or broken, that keep them stuck. But when we meet them with connection and compassion, we help them feel the love they've been missing. That's when we can finally break old patterns and move forward with more kindness and self-acceptance.

Too Much or Never Enough

If you often feel like you're "too much" or "not enough," know this: your sensitivity, awareness, and emotional depth are strengths, not weaknesses. People who struggle with these feelings tend to be highly sensitive and perceptive, often taking on the tough work of breaking generational cycles of trauma. While this journey can stir up resistance and shame from others, it leads to profound growth and fulfillment.

Your ability to connect with your emotions and intuition is a gift, even if it feels overwhelming to those who aren't as in touch with their own feelings. By embracing the parts of yourself you've distanced yourself from and untangling shame from your experiences, you'll find that your intuition, emotional resilience, and sensitivity become powerful tools. Sure, some people may find you "too much," and others may make you feel like "not enough," but the more you trust and honor your sensitivity, the less those old narratives will have power over you.

Unburdening your parts is about getting to know them on a deeper level and understanding the positive intentions behind their actions. Each part—whether it's trying to protect you or shield your pain—has been carrying a heavy load to keep you safe. To help them let go of that weight, approach them with curiosity, not judgment. If you feel frustrated, ashamed, or fearful, that's just another part stepping in. By staying compassionate and open, you create a safe space for these parts to release the roles they've been stuck in.

When parts begin to unburden, your protectors don't have to react so intensely anymore, giving you more freedom and clarity in how you navigate life. You'll notice less internal conflict and tension, making it easier to respond to situations with a greater sense of choice. I won't go into the whole methodology here, but a good place to start is by "part mapping"—taking a step back and observing how your parts are behaving, what they need, and which one seems to be calling the shots. This gentle exploration helps you understand your inner world and creates space for deeper healing. I've included this as a discovery prompt at the end of the chapter.

Putting it all Together - Carmen's Story

Background

Carmen, a 32-year-old entrepreneur, is known for her fierce independence. She built her business from the ground up and prides herself on handling everything alone, rarely asking for help. On the outside, she seems strong and self-reliant, but inside, Carmen feels lonely and overwhelmed. Through our work together, she started to uncover a deeper issue behind her need for independence—a core belief from her Exile that said: "I need to be fiercely independent and can't rely on anyone else."

The Exile: Fear of Dependence

Carmen's Exile formed early in her childhood when she learned that depending on others often led to disappointment. Growing up with emotionally distant parents, she internalized the belief that relying on others would only result in being let down or rejected. This Exile carried the fear that trusting others made her vulnerable, so to protect herself, Carmen believed she must always handle things on her own. This part of her held onto the idea that self-reliance was the only way to stay safe, leaving her emotionally isolated.

The Managers: Emotional Guarding and Control

Carmen's Managers stepped in to protect her from the pain of feeling vulnerable. One Manager kept her emotionally guarded, making sure she avoided relying on others in her relationships. This part worked by keeping Carmen emotionally distant from people, ensuring she didn't get hurt. Another Manager ensured Carmen stayed busy and in control of her life. These parts believed that as long as she didn't ask for help and kept things running smoothly on her own, she wouldn't feel the rejection her Exile feared. However, this constant emotional guarding left Carmen feeling isolated and disconnected from those around her.

The Firefighters: Excessive Drinking and Emotional Numbing

When the pressure of isolation and self-reliance became too much, Carmen's Firefighters rushed in to help her escape the emotional burden. Her most active Firefighter encouraged excessive drinking as a way to numb her feelings of loneliness and stress. After a tough day, Carmen often turned to alcohol, finding temporary relief from the emotional pain she tried so hard to suppress. The Firefighter saw drinking as an effective way to shut down the overwhelming emotions that surfaced when Carmen's independence became too heavy to bear.

The drinking, while providing a brief escape, often left Carmen feeling guilty and ashamed afterward, reinforcing her belief that she can't rely on anyone else and must carry everything herself. This cycle of numbing and regret made it harder for Carmen to address the root cause of her pain—the Exile's fear of depending on others.

Healing

Through our work together, Carmen began to recognize the role her Exile played in her life and the fear that drove her need to be independent. By offering compassion and understanding to this wounded part, she started to challenge the belief that she must handle everything alone.

At the same time, Carmen began to address the role of her Firefighter's excessive drinking. With healthier coping mechanisms, Carmen learned to manage her emotions without needing to numb them. Over time, she found more balance, realizing that sharing her struggles didn't make her vulnerable—it allowed her to feel supported and connected. This process helped Carmen overcome the isolation her independence once created, leading to a more fulfilling and connected life.

Discovery Prompt: Part Mapping

A good place to start identifying your parts is by "part mapping"—taking a step back and observing how your parts are behaving, what they need, and which one seems to be calling the shots. This gentle exploration helps you understand your inner world and creates space for deeper healing.

This exercise is designed to help you recognize the different parts that operate within you. By getting familiar with how each of these parts works, you'll gain deeper insight into the ways they protect you and the wounds they're shielding.

Step 1: Spot Your Managers

Your managers are the proactive parts that keep things in check. They push you to manage, plan, or perfect your environment, often to avoid emotional discomfort. Reflect on these questions:

1. *What behaviors do you lean on to maintain control or sidestep uncomfortable feelings?* (e.g., overworking, people-pleasing, striving for perfection)
2. *What are these parts protecting you from?* (e.g., fear of failure, rejection, or criticism)
3. *How did these parts help you when you were younger?* (e.g., keeping peace at home, avoiding conflict)

Example: "I push myself hard at work because my manager parts believe that if I don't succeed, I'll be seen as a failure."

Step 2: Spot Your Firefighters

Firefighters are your reactive parts—they jump in when emotions run high. They might distract you or help you numb out when things feel overwhelming. Ask yourself:

1. *What behaviors do you turn to for quick relief when you're stressed or upset?* (e.g., binge-watching TV, scrolling on social media, drinking, procrastinating)

2. *What emotions are these firefighters trying to manage?* (e.g., shame, fear, anxiety)

3. *How have these parts protected you during emotionally intense times?*

Example: "When I feel criticized, my firefighter takes over by binge-watching TV to escape the feeling of inadequacy."

Step 3: Spot Your Exiles ("inner child")

Your exiles are the vulnerable pieces of you that hold onto past pain—often tied to early life experiences. These parts carry emotions like shame, fear, or loneliness, and your managers and firefighters work overtime to keep those feelings buried. Reflect on:

1. *What deeper feelings of unworthiness or shame sit beneath your manager or firefighter behaviors?* (e.g., "I'm unlovable," "I don't matter," "I'm not enough")

2. *Can you recall a time in childhood when you first felt this way?* (e.g., being ignored, criticized, or left out)

3. *What does this wounded part need from you now?* (e.g., acknowledgment, compassion, reassurance, validation)

Example: "I remember feeling invisible when my parents didn't come to my school play. That part of me still feels unimportant when I'm overlooked."

Step 4: Connect the Dots

Take a moment to reflect on how your parts interact:

1. *How do your managers and firefighters work together to keep your exiles hidden?* (e.g., "My manager keeps me busy so I don't have to feel lonely, but when those feelings sneak in, my firefighter distracts me with TV.")

2. *How do your protective parts feel about their roles?* (e.g., tired, overwhelmed, stuck in constant defense mode)

3. *Can you acknowledge and thank your managers and firefighters for their efforts, while offering your exiles the care they need?*

Reflection: "I see that my drive for perfection at work is my manager trying to protect me from failure, and my binge-watching is my firefighter's way of numbing the fear. Both are working to protect my exile that feels deeply unworthy."

By recognizing how these parts operate, you can start to relieve some of their burden, leading to a more peaceful and compassionate inner world.

CHAPTER 11

Mind-Body Connection

O ur brains are not static. They're dynamic, adaptable, and constantly evolving. This built-in ability to rewire and reshape itself means that the beliefs and patterns we've come to see as unshakable truths are anything but permanent. They can be shifted, expanded, and replaced with new perspectives. This incredible flexibility is the foundation for rewiring the core beliefs that no longer serve us, giving us the power to create a reality that aligns more closely with our goals and values.

We first need to understand how the brain works in tandem with the body to shape how we perceive and respond to the world. The brain doesn't operate in isolation—it's deeply intertwined with the nervous system, constantly exchanging signals about our internal and external experiences. This intricate feedback loop forms the mind-body connection, a vital relationship that influences how we think, feel, and act.

As part of this ongoing dialogue, the brain relies on tools like neuroception and interoception to make sense of the world and assess safety. Neuroception is the brain's subconscious scanning of the environment for signs of threat or safety, while interoception is our awareness of internal bodily sensations—like the tightness in your chest before a big presentation or the soothing rhythm of your breath when you're at ease. When these processes fall out of balance, we can lose touch with our bodies, leading to a state called disembodiment, which often leaves us feeling disconnected or stuck in unproductive mental loops.

Another lens for understanding the brain's complexity lies in the relationship between the right and left hemispheres. The right brain, often linked with creativity, emotion, and intuition, works in tandem with the left brain, which specializes in logic, structure, and analysis. Together, these hemispheres shape our perceptions and behaviors. But when one side dominates, imbalance can occur. Restoring harmony between these hemispheres—and reconnecting with the body—opens the door to greater resilience, clarity, and alignment.

In this chapter, we'll explore these concepts and uncover how the brain's adaptability makes it possible to rewrite outdated beliefs. Together, we'll build a foundation for crafting an updated narrative—one thought, one connection, one rewired belief at a time.

Neuroplasticity

Thoughts can be learned and unlearned. Neuroplasticity is the brain's incredible ability to change and adapt, no matter how old we are. For a long time, people believed our brains were "set" after childhood, but science now shows that our brains are always forming new connections. Whether we're learning something new, building healthier habits, or even recovering from setbacks, our brains are constantly evolving. This means we have far more power to shape our minds than we ever thought possible.

This adaptability also applies to our core beliefs—the deeply held ideas we have about ourselves and the world. These beliefs, formed early in life, can feel like permanent fixtures, but thanks to neuroplasticity, they're not set in stone. By questioning negative or limiting beliefs and focusing intentionally on more positive perspectives, we can literally retrain our brains to think differently. With enough repetition and consistency, those healthier thoughts can start to feel more natural, while the old patterns begin to fade.

For example, if someone has always believed they're not good enough, they can start to challenge that by paying attention to their strengths and accomplishments, even the small ones. Over time, as they consistently practice thinking in a more positive way, their brain starts reinforcing those new beliefs, making them feel more true and automatic. It's not just about shifting your mindset once or twice—it's about turning those new thoughts into a habit, so the brain prioritizes them.

In other words, neuroplasticity gives us the power to rewrite our mental stories. We're not stuck with the thoughts and beliefs we've always had—we can reshape them. It's a hopeful reminder that real, lasting change is possible if we're willing to put in the effort. Our brains are more flexible than we think, and with persistence, we can create a mindset that truly supports who we want to become, even if we don't fully believe those things yet.

Omar's Story

Omar grew up in a modest neighborhood in a bustling city, the middle child of five siblings. His parents worked long hours, and while they provided for the family financially, emotional support was scarce. Omar's father was a hard-working man, but his praise was minimal. Mistakes, even minor ones, were met with criticism, and Omar internalized a core belief early in life: *"I'm not good enough."*

At school, despite his efforts to succeed, Omar struggled with this belief. Even when he performed well, he felt that his achievements weren't significant. Compliments from teachers or peers felt hollow because they didn't align with his deeply ingrained view of himself. His inner dialogue constantly echoed, *"I'll never be good enough, no matter what I do."*

This belief permeated other areas of his life as well. In friendships, he often felt like a burden, assuming people tolerated him rather than genuinely liking him. In relationships, he would shy away from vulnerability, fearing that if people really knew him, they would confirm his worst fear: that he wasn't worthy of love or respect.

By his mid-20s, Omar became aware that this pattern was holding him back. No matter how much he achieved in his career or how supportive people around him were, his mind kept reverting to the belief that he didn't measure up. Realizing the impact of this, Omar sought me out for therapy.

During our work together, Omar noticed subtle but significant changes. Initially, when faced with failure or criticism, his instinct was still to revert to old patterns, but now he had the tools to counter them. The more he practiced new thought patterns, the easier it became to believe in his worth. His brain, through neuroplasticity, was literally rewiring itself to support these new beliefs.

New neural pathways were formed that allowed positive experiences to be processed differently. Instead of brushing off compliments or attributing success to luck, Omar began internalizing these positive events, recognizing his role in achieving them. As his brain continued to strengthen these new connections, the old belief—*"I'm not good enough"*—started to lose its grip on him.

He also began to engage more fully in his relationships. No longer assuming that he was a burden, he opened up to his friends and family, who responded with genuine warmth and appreciation. This, in turn, reinforced his new belief of *"I have value and self-worth."*

Over time, Omar's new belief became firmly rooted. While the old thought of not being good enough still appeared occasionally, it no longer had the power it once did. He could recognize it as an echo of his past, not as an inherent truth about himself.

Neuroception

The stories we tell ourselves about our experiences come directly from the state our nervous system is in at that moment. When something happens—whether it's a stressful situation or just a small interaction—our nervous system reacts first, often before we even have a chance to think about it. This is because our body is always scanning for signs of safety or danger, a process called neuroception. Once our nervous system picks up on something, it shifts into a state—like fight, flight, or rest—and that state shapes our emotions, reactions, and ultimately the story we create about what's going on. As Deb Dana (2018) says, "story follows state," meaning the way we interpret an event is deeply influenced by what's happening inside our nervous system at the time.

If our nervous system senses danger, even if there's no real threat, we can quickly slip into "fight or flight" mode. In that state, everything feels urgent or overwhelming, and the story we tell ourselves might be full of anxiety, anger, or a need to protect ourselves. But if we're feeling safe and calm, the story shifts—we feel more open, trusting, and grounded. Our thoughts and behaviors in that state reflect peace and connection rather than survival mode.

The phrase "story follows state" reminds us that the narratives we create aren't always a reflection of reality, but rather of how our nervous system is reacting in that moment. Our past experiences shape this, forming what's called a personal neural profile. This means that if you've been through a lot of stress or trauma, your nervous system might be on high alert more often, making you feel like you're in danger even when everything is fine. As a result, you might find yourself stuck in cycles of fear, worry, or mistrust, even in safe situations.

But once you begin to understand your own nervous system— what triggers you and what helps you feel safe—you can start to separate your state from your story. You'll begin to realize that maybe it's not the situation that's the problem, but the state your body is in when it happens. Learning to track these states gives you the power to change your responses. You can calm your nervous system and, over time, rewrite the stories you tell yourself from a place of peace, not fear.

Have you ever walked into a room and just felt like something was off, even though you couldn't explain why? Or maybe you've been in a conversation where someone gave you an "icky" feeling, but you couldn't quite pinpoint what caused it. You might've noticed yourself fidgeting or tapping your foot nervously before you even realized you were anxious. These are your body's ways of picking up on things and trying to clue you in on what's happening beneath the surface.

Our bodies are always sensing and reacting to the world around us, often before our minds catch up. In a culture that places so much value on logical thinking—asking questions like "What did I see?" or "What's the evidence?"—we can easily overlook another key source of information: our body's own wisdom. It's constantly giving us signals about how we're really feeling, if we take the time to listen.

Kendra's Story

Kendra, now 38 years old, grew up as the youngest of three children in a small Midwest town. Her early years were marked by uncertainty due to the constant conflict between her mother and older sister, who lived with undiagnosed Bipolar Disorder. The emotional volatility in the household created an environment of tension and unpredictability. Her mother, overwhelmed and ill-equipped to manage her sister's mood swings, oscillated between frustration and withdrawal, leaving Kendra and her other siblings to navigate the emotional chaos on their own.

By age eight, Kendra's body had become attuned to the smallest signs of impending conflict. A slammed door, a sudden change in her sister's tone, or the sound of her mother's exasperated sighs would send her heart racing, her mind bracing for the worst. At school, she was described as bright but quiet, often startling at loud noises. She laughed it off, but her body remained in a constant state of readiness, always prepared for the next emotional eruption at home.

As a teenager, she became a peacekeeper, anticipating others' needs and smoothing over conflicts, but it came at a cost. Beneath her calm exterior, she was always on high alert, monitoring the emotional climate around her to prevent outbursts before they began. College brought independence, but her body's ingrained hyper-awareness followed her. Crowds, loud noises, and sudden changes often left her overwhelmed, and she sought refuge in quiet spaces where she could regain a sense of control.

In adulthood, Kendra's ability to predict and manage crises made her a successful project manager, but it stemmed from the same heightened vigilance that had protected her as a child. Through therapy, she learned to regulate her nervous system, becoming more attuned to her body's responses. She practiced mindfulness techniques, deep breathing, and grounding exercises, helping her recognize when her body was slipping into fight-or-flight mode. Gradually, she learned to calm herself before the response spiraled, gaining greater control over her reactions and finding moments of peace.

Kendra created a peaceful home for her own family, breaking the cycle of tension she grew up in. Although her past left its mark, she became a resilient and compassionate woman, known for her ability to remain calm under pressure and her deep empathy for others.

Right Brain vs. Left Brain

Our right brain plays a crucial role in connecting us to our bodies and deeply influences how we experience and process emotions. Unlike the left brain, which is more focused on logic and language, the right brain is responsible for our emotional experiences, creativity, and intuition. It's also where we process nonverbal cues and bodily sensations, making it a key player in how we perceive and respond to the world around us. This side of the brain is closely linked to our body's physical states, allowing us to feel our emotions in a visceral, embodied way.

When we experience emotions, it's the right brain that helps us tune into the physical sensations that come with them. For example, the tightness in your chest when you're anxious or the warmth in your heart when you feel love is processed through the right brain's connection to your body. This connection allows emotions to become more than just thoughts in our minds—they turn into full-body experiences that affect how we move, breathe, and interact with others. When we're in tune with our right brain, we're better able to notice and stay present with these sensations, which makes it easier to understand and process our emotions.

But when we're disconnected from our right brain or overly reliant on the left brain's logical processes, we can lose touch with these important bodily signals. This disconnection makes it harder to identify what we're truly feeling and why. It can also lead to suppressing emotions, as we try to think our way through problems rather than feeling our way through them. This is where practices like interoception—tuning into and describing bodily sensations—become so valuable.

Many people, especially those who are more analytically minded, tend to intellectualize their emotions—approaching feelings as problems to solve rather than experiences to feel. Instead of connecting with their emotions on a visceral level, they analyze and dissect them logically, keeping everything in their heads. It's like holding a balloon—your head—completely detached from your body. You can look at it, study it, even try to control it, but there's no grounded connection to your physical, lived experience. This disconnection makes it hard to fully process emotions, leaving them floating unresolved while your body continues to carry the weight of what your mind is working so hard to avoid.

Understanding the role of the right brain in our emotional life reminds us that emotions aren't just mental—they're deeply physical, too. By nurturing our connection to the right brain and our bodies, we can cultivate a more balanced, compassionate approach to our emotions, ultimately building a deeper sense of self-awareness and emotional resilience.

Interoception

Interoception is the practice of tuning into your body's internal signals—learning to notice and stay present with your physical sensations. It's like learning a new language—the language of your nervous system. By focusing on how emotions show up as physical sensations in your body, you can interrupt the mental chatter and looping thoughts that often keep emotions trapped inside. This process starts with simple awareness: scanning your body and asking yourself questions like, "Where do I feel this?" "Is it moving or still?" or "Does it have a temperature, color, or texture?" These questions help ground you in the present moment, allowing you to connect more deeply with what you're truly feeling.

Throughout the day, we often get stuck in our heads, replaying situations on a loop. To break this automatic pattern, try setting a reminder on your phone a few times a day to check in with your body. Take a moment to scan your body, and notice what you're feeling. Then, breathe into that sensation. Imagine sending compassion to the area where you feel the emotion most strongly. The goal isn't to judge or fix the sensation, but simply to allow it to exist as it is. By befriending these sensations, you let the emotions move through you instead of getting stuck.

No emotion is inherently good or bad; they're just messages from your body, reflecting unmet needs. For example, anger might be telling you to speak up, while sadness could signal a need for comfort. By identifying and labeling these sensations, you engage your logical mind, which helps you regulate your emotions more effectively. This practice of "naming it to tame it" (a phrase coined by Dr. Dan Siegel) allows you to process what you're feeling and respond in a more balanced way.

As you build your interoceptive skills, use self-validating affirmations to strengthen your connection to your body. Remind yourself that it's okay to feel whatever you're feeling without needing to explain or change it. Affirmations like "All my feelings are welcome here" or "It's okay for me to feel this way" help create a sense of safety and acceptance within yourself.

Discovery Prompt: Addressing ANTs

This exercise focuses on identifying and challenging Automatic Negative Thoughts (ANTs)—those quick, reflexive thoughts that often distort reality. By recognizing and replacing ANTs, you can develop healthier mental patterns and harness neuroplasticity to retrain your brain.

Step 1: Spot Your ANTs

Automatic Negative Thoughts are unhelpful mental habits that influence your emotions and behaviors. Reflect on a recent situation that triggered strong negative emotions and consider:

1. **What thoughts immediately popped into your mind?**
   (e.g., "I'm a failure," "They don't care about me.")

2. **What emotions followed these thoughts?**
   (e.g., sadness, frustration, anxiety.)

3. **What type of ANTs might these represent?**
   - *All-or-Nothing ANT:* "If I don't succeed completely, I've failed."
   - *Catastrophic ("What if") ANT:* "What if this is a complete disaster?"
   - *Mind-Reading ANT:* "They think I'm incompetent."
   - *Personalizing ANT:* "This problem is entirely my fault."

Example: "When my friend didn't text me back, I thought, 'They must be mad at me.' This triggered anxiety and guilt. It's an example of a Mind-Reading ANT."

Step 2: Challenge Your ANTs

Once you've identified the ANTs, it's time to challenge their accuracy. Use these questions to shift your perspective:

1. **What evidence supports this ANT?**

   (e.g., "They didn't reply to my text right away.")

2. **What evidence contradicts this ANT?**

   (e.g., "They've been busy before but weren't upset with me. They might just be busy now.")

3. **What's a more realistic, balanced thought?**

   (e.g., "There could be many reasons they didn't reply—it doesn't mean they're upset with me.")

Example: "My ANT was, 'They must be mad at me,' but when I looked at the evidence, I realized I had no proof. A more realistic thought is, 'They're probably busy, and I'll hear from them soon.'"

Step 3: Reframe and Replace

Replacing ANTs involves creating new, empowering thoughts that feel true and actionable. Reflect on:

1. **What would I say to a friend who had this ANT?**

   (e.g., "Don't jump to conclusions; they might just be having a busy day.")

2. **How does this new thought make me feel?**

   (e.g., "I feel more calm and less anxious.")

3. **What action can I take to reinforce this new thought?**

   (e.g., "Instead of ruminating, I'll focus on something else until I hear from them.")

Example: "I restructured my ANT from 'They're mad at me' to 'They're probably busy.' This made me feel calmer, and I decided to go for a walk instead of overthinking."

Step 4: Reflect and Integrate

1. **What patterns are emerging in your ANTs?**

   (e.g., "I often jump to conclusions or assume the worst.")

2. **How does reframing ANTs change your emotions and behaviors?**

   (e.g., "I feel less anxious and more empowered to act constructively.")

3. **What steps can you take to reinforce this practice moving forward?**

   (e.g., "I'll set aside time weekly to reflect on my progress and identify any persistent ANTs.")

By addressing and reframing ANTs, you are retraining your brain to respond more constructively to challenges. Over time, this practice strengthens positive neural pathways, reducing the grip of negative thought patterns and enhancing your emotional well-being.

CHAPTER 12

Your Nervous System

E ver notice your heart pounding in panic, your breath quickening with tension, or a strange detachment taking over when stress becomes overwhelming? These sensations aren't random—they're your nervous system at work, an intricate design built to keep you safe and adaptive in a constantly shifting world. It's your body's command center. Long before you were aware of it, your nervous system was learning how to respond to the world based on your earliest experiences. It developed patterns to navigate the safety or danger it perceived in your environment, laying the groundwork for the states you move through today.

But here's the twist: sometimes the sensations in our body come first, and then our mind steps in to explain them. For instance, if your nervous system learned to remain hypervigilant as a child—always scanning for potential threats—it might trigger a tight chest or racing thoughts when you encounter something mildly stressful. Your brain, trying to make sense of this, might interpret those feelings as evidence that "I'm not good enough" or "I can't handle this," reinforcing negative core beliefs. These beliefs, once formed, feed back into the nervous system, keeping you stuck in cycles of stress and self-doubt.

How we interpret our physical reactions can either build us up or tear us down. Over time, these interpretations stack up and contribute to our core beliefs and self-schemas. If we consistently view our physical responses negatively, it can solidify harmful beliefs about ourselves and the world around us. For instance, someone who frequently feels anxious in social settings might begin to believe they're unlikable or socially inept, interpreting their anxiety as evidence. This creates a cycle that's tough to break—where negative interpretations reinforce negative core beliefs.

By paying attention to how we label our physical responses, and how much power our thoughts have in shaping our feelings and self-perception, we can begin to challenge and change those automatic negative thoughts (ANTS). This shift allows us to manage emotions more effectively, build healthier self-schemas, and create core beliefs that are more positive and empowering. Realizing that our emotions are a mix of both body and mind gives us a powerful tool for improving emotional well-being and personal growth.

Understanding this connection is where the Polyvagal Theory, developed by Dr. Stephen Porges, comes into play. This theory explains how our nervous system operates through a hierarchy of states—fight or flight, immobilization, freeze, or fawn—based on the patterns it learned growing up. These states are not just reactions to stress; they shape how we connect, protect, and survive. At the heart of it all is the vagus nerve, the body's main communicator between brain and body, which governs these responses and influences both our emotional and physical experiences. And here's the important part: these responses aren't weaknesses. They're evidence of a nervous system that adapted as best it could to your past, even if those adaptations no longer serve you.

The Vagus Nerve

The vagus nerve is like the body's "calm button," playing a huge role in how we handle stress & emotions. It's the longest nerve in the body, running from the brain all the way down to the stomach, connecting with key organs like the heart and lungs. Its main job is to help us relax and recover after stress. When the vagus nerve is activated, it keeps us feeling calm, steadying our heart rate, and even supporting digestion. Essentially, it's the nerve that tells our body, "Hey, it's okay to chill out now."

After a stressful situation, the vagus nerve helps bring us back to a peaceful state. This ability to calm down after stress is known as "vagal tone"—think of it like a muscle. If you have strong vagal tone, you can bounce back from stress more easily—you feel more emotionally balanced and resilient. But if your vagal tone is low, it's like getting stuck in stress mode, leading to feelings of anxiety, low mood, or even issues with digestion and sleep. In short, the vagus nerve helps us move out of survival mode and back into feeling safe and grounded.

The vagus nerve also plays a big part in how we feel emotionally and socially. It helps us pick up on other people's emotions and feel connected to them, which is why it's so important for relationships. When we feel safe with someone, the vagus nerve helps keep us calm and connected. But if we feel threatened, it can push us into anxiety or make us shut down and pull away. This shows that the vagus nerve isn't just about physical health—it's also deeply tied to how we experience emotions and connect with others.

Our core beliefs—the deep-down things we believe about ourselves and the world—are closely linked to how the vagus nerve works. If you believe the world is unsafe or that you constantly need to be on guard, your vagus nerve might stay on high alert, making it harder to relax and feel at ease. But if you believe you can handle challenges and that the world isn't always out to get you, your vagus nerve helps you stay calm, even when things get tough. This connection between what we believe and how our body responds is a powerful reminder of how closely our mind and body are linked.

The Language of Stress

Polyvagal theory, created by Dr. Stephen Porges, and based on the vagus nerve, goes a step further in explaining how our nervous system responds to stress and shapes how we feel and act. Essentially, our nervous system operates in one of three states: a calm, connected state; a fight-or-flight state; or a shutdown state. These states influence how we interact with the world, especially when we feel safe or threatened. Our bodies are constantly scanning for signs of danger or safety, and depending on what they pick up, we move between these three states.

The first state is the *ventral vagal state*, where we feel safe, grounded, and connected to others. In this state, we're calm, able to think clearly, engage with people, and feel at ease in our environment. This is our "rest-and-digest" mode, where our nervous system is balanced, and we feel comfortable. Being around supportive friends, feeling secure, or being in a peaceful environment can keep us in this state. When we're here, life feels manageable, and we're open to connection.

The second state is the *sympathetic state*, which kicks in when we sense danger. This is the well-known "fight-or-flight" mode. In "fight," we respond with anger or frustration, ready to confront whatever we feel is threatening us. For example, if you feel disrespected, you might snap back or become defensive. "Flight," on the other hand, is driven by fear or anxiety, making you want to avoid or escape the situation. Think of that nervous energy when you want to get out of a stressful environment, like a crowded room where you feel judged or overwhelmed. Your body prepares to either fight or flee.

The third state is the *dorsal vagal state*, which happens when we feel completely overwhelmed or powerless. This is the "freeze" or "shutdown" mode, where it feels like there's no way to fight or escape, so the body just shuts down to protect itself. You might feel emotionally numb or detached, like checking out mentally because everything feels like too much. Triggers for this state might include long-term stress, trauma, or situations where you feel stuck, like being in a toxic relationship or a draining job. In this state, it's hard to engage with life because it feels like there's no way out.

These three states—*ventral vagal* (feeling safe), *sympathetic* (fight/flight), and *dorsal vagal* (shutdown)—show how our nervous system reacts to the world around us. They help explain why sometimes we feel connected and calm, and other times anxious, angry, or completely drained. Understanding these states can help us manage stress and recognize what's going on inside when we're feeling overwhelmed.

Fight or Flight (Hyperarousal)

We've all heard of the fight-or-flight response - the instinct that kicks in when we feel threatened. Whether the danger is real or just perceived, our body goes into overdrive to protect us. This is called hyperarousal. It's like your body shifts into high gear, preparing you to either confront the threat (fight) or escape it (flight). You might notice your heart racing, your muscles tensing, or a general feeling of being on edge, even when there's no real danger in front of you. It's like being stuck in a constant state of readiness.

In hyperarousal, the world feels unsafe, and even small stressors can trigger waves of anxiety or restlessness. You might find yourself always anticipating the next problem, never fully able to relax. Your body stays on high alert, convinced that something bad is just around the corner. This constant state of vigilance can be exhausting, both mentally and physically. You might struggle to sleep, have trouble focusing, or feel easily irritated. It's as if your nervous system has forgotten how to wind down.

A lot of this response comes from the beliefs we hold. If you've grown up feeling like the world is a dangerous place, your nervous system adapts by staying in this fight-or-flight mode. Over time, you might even start to believe that this constant state of stress is just who you are. But in reality, it's your body trying to protect you—even when the threat isn't really there.

Recognizing when you're in hyperarousal is the first step toward getting unstuck. By focusing on calming your body first, you can begin to shift out of that high-gear state. It's about teaching your nervous system that it's safe to relax, even if your mind is still stuck in stress mode. The more you engage your body in this process, the easier it becomes to find a sense of balance again.

Ethan's Story

Ethan, a 51-year-old civil engineer, grew up in a household where tension and criticism were constant. His father had a quick temper and unpredictable moods, while his mother often avoided conflict by withdrawing. As the middle child, Ethan frequently bore the brunt of his father's anger, whether it was for minor mistakes or perceived slights. Over time, Ethan developed a "fight response" to cope with the chaos in his home, channeling his fear and frustration into anger as a way to protect himself and assert control in an environment where he often felt powerless.

Reacting to stress with defensiveness, frustration, or aggression became Ethan's default. As a child, he quickly learned that showing vulnerability or fear would only invite more criticism. Instead, he met conflict with anger, yelling back at his father or lashing out at his siblings when tensions escalated. This approach, while instinctive, helped Ethan feel a sense of power in situations where he otherwise felt small and helpless. However, it also reinforced his belief that the only way to protect himself was to stay on the offensive, making him quick to anger and defensive when challenged.

In school, Ethan's quick temper and low frustration tolerance led to frequent outbursts, isolating him from peers and teachers. While his assertiveness was sometimes seen as strength, it masked a deeper fear of rejection and inadequacy. He struggled to form close relationships, dismissing feedback as criticism and reinforcing his belief that defensiveness was necessary for self-protection. These patterns carried into adulthood, where Ethan's fight response created challenges in his romantic relationships and career. Arguments with partners often escalated, and his volatile reactions at work strained collaborations despite his talent.

Ethan recognized the toll his anger was taking on his personal and professional life and sought out therapy. Together, we explored how his fight response had developed as a survival strategy in childhood, helping him understand that his reactions were not flaws but learned behaviors. This insight allowed Ethan to address the triggers behind his anger and reframe vulnerability as a strength rather than a weakness. He began to challenge deeply held beliefs about defensiveness and practice pausing before reacting.

As Ethan rewired his nervous system and adopted new coping strategies, his relationships improved. He communicated more openly with his partner, fostering trust and understanding, and his colleagues noticed a more collaborative and composed demeanor at work. While moments of frustration still arose, Ethan learned to manage his emotions constructively, viewing feedback as an opportunity for growth instead of a threat.

Collapse/Immobilized (Hypoarousal)

The collapse or immobilized state is the body's way of shutting down when things feel too overwhelming to handle. In moments of extreme danger or stress, it's like your body decides the best way to protect you is to disconnect and shut off, so you don't have to feel the full intensity of what's happening. This isn't something you consciously choose—it's an automatic response when your nervous system doesn't see any other way out.

Even though it can feel strange or frustrating, it's your body's way of looking out for you.

When you're in this state, your muscles go limp, and it feels like all your energy is drained. Your heart rate and breathing slow down, and you might feel distant or spaced out, as if you're not fully present. You may struggle to speak or focus on what's happening around you. It's like your body and mind go on autopilot, trying to protect you by numbing you to the pain or fear of the moment.

This reaction is actually the body's last defense when it feels like there's no way to fight or escape. It releases natural painkillers to help you disconnect from the situation, so you might feel emotionally or physically numb. Even though it can feel disorienting, it's important to understand that your body is doing its best to shield you in a difficult situation.

Afterward, it's common to feel confused or find it hard to make sense of what happened because your mind wasn't fully present. Processing this can be challenging, but knowing that your body was trying to help you can be comforting. Understanding this response allows you to be gentle with yourself as you work through the aftermath.

Freeze (Blended)

The freeze response is your body's way of hitting the brakes when everything feels too overwhelming to handle. It's that moment when you feel stuck, numb, or completely disconnected from what's going on around you. Your brain decides that fighting back or running away isn't an option, so it freezes, trying to protect you by shutting down emotionally or physically. In that state, it's hard to think, move, or make decisions—it's like you're paralyzed, unable to take action.

What makes freezing different is that your body is still full of nervous energy, as if it's gearing up for fight or flight, but at the same time, it's unable to release that energy. You might feel your muscles tense, your heart race, and your body bracing for action, but you can't move. It's like being caught in a tug-of-war between wanting to react and being stuck in place, leaving you frozen and unable to move forward.

This response is a survival tactic—your body's way of making you invisible to a threat. But when you get stuck in freeze mode, it can be hard to feel present in your own life. You might feel disconnected from yourself and the people around you, struggling to make even small decisions or take basic steps. The tension builds in your body, but with no way to release it, everything feels overwhelming.

Even after the danger has passed, your body may be ready to jump back into action, but staying stuck in that frozen state makes it hard to shake off the tension. You can feel trapped, even when the threat is gone. Learning to recognize when you're in a freeze response can help you start to slowly regain control and move forward again.

Fawn (Blended)

The fawn response happens when, instead of freezing or fighting, you cope with feeling unsafe by trying to make others happy. You go out of your way to avoid conflict, agreeing with people—even when it's not what you really want—just to keep the peace. In situations where you feel powerless, it feels easier and safer to please everyone rather than risk an argument or rejection. This often shows up in relationships where it seems like your needs don't matter as much as keeping things smooth and avoiding confrontation.

When you're stuck in the fawn response, it's hard to stay connected to yourself. You might constantly put others first, to the point where you lose track of what *you* actually want or need. It's like you're hyper-focused on everyone else's emotions but completely out of touch with your own. Over time, this can leave you feeling drained, exhausted, and unsure of who you really are, because you're always bending over backwards to make sure others are okay.

In this state, you become really good at reading the emotions and needs of others, adjusting your behavior to avoid upsetting them. But as you do this, you start disconnecting from your own body and feelings. It can feel like you're living in a fog or that things around you aren't fully real. The constant effort to keep others happy while ignoring your own needs can wear you down, leaving you feeling both mentally and physically exhausted.

Over time, this pattern can turn into people-pleasing, where you struggle to say no or set boundaries because you're so focused on keeping everyone else content. You might apologize constantly, feel like you don't know who you are, and have a hard time prioritizing yourself. Recognizing this response is the first step toward breaking this cycle and learning how to reconnect with your own needs and set boundaries that work for you.

Alex's Story

Alex, a 44-year-old financial consultant, grew up with a narcissistic mother who always made him feel as though his needs were secondary to her own. His childhood was spent trying to earn his mother's approval, constantly adjusting his behavior to avoid her anger or dissatisfaction. His mother had a way of turning every conversation back to herself, and whenever Alex expressed a need or emotion, it was met with dismissal or criticism. Over time, Alex learned that the easiest way to keep the peace was to agree with her and make her happy, no matter how much it cost him emotionally. This pattern developed into what is known as the "fawn response"—a survival mechanism where Alex coped with feelings of powerlessness by becoming overly accommodating.

Now, as an adult, Alex still finds himself defaulting to this fawn response, especially in his personal and professional relationships. Whether it's his demanding boss or his partner, Alex has trouble setting boundaries and frequently puts the needs of others ahead of his own. In social situations, he goes out of his way to keep everyone happy, avoiding confrontation at all costs. He constantly agrees with others, even when it's not what he really wants, because deep down, he fears rejection or criticism. The habit of people-pleasing has become so ingrained in him that Alex struggles to even identify what his own desires or boundaries are anymore.

This pattern has left Alex feeling mentally and physically drained. He's become highly attuned to the emotions and needs of those around him, often sensing when someone is upset or dissatisfied. To avoid conflict, he quickly shifts his behavior to make sure they're content, but this constant vigilance has taken a toll on his emotional health. Alex feels disconnected from his own needs, living in a fog where everything feels slightly unreal. His focus is so often on pleasing others that he has lost touch with his own identity, unsure of who he really is or what he truly wants. The exhaustion of always bending to meet the needs of others has left him feeling empty and burnt out.

Over time, Alex's inability to say no or set boundaries led to deep resentment and self-neglect. He frequently apologized, even when he hadn't done anything wrong, and felt guilty if he prioritized himself. Recognizing that his fawn response stemmed from his childhood experiences with his narcissistic mother was a crucial first step for Alex to start breaking this pattern. By beginning to reconnect with his own needs and learning how to set healthy boundaries, Alex slowly worked toward a life where he could balance his desire to maintain peace with his right to care for himself.

Discovery Prompt: How State Shapes Story

In Polyvagal Theory, the phrase "story follows state" highlights how our nervous system shapes the way we interpret events. When we're calm, our stories tend to be more balanced and grounded. But when we're stressed or shut down, our thoughts often become more negative or reactive. This exercise is designed to help you explore how the state of your nervous system influences the story you tell yourself about your experience.

Step 1: Recall a Recent Situation

Think of a recent event in which you experienced a strong emotional reaction—whether positive or negative. It could be an interaction with someone, a stressful moment at work, or even a situation in which you felt disconnected or overwhelmed.

Step 2: Tune Into Your Nervous System's Response

Reflect on how your body reacted during the event:

1. What was the situation? Describe it briefly.
2. What state was your nervous system in? (use the Polyvagal states from this chapter):
   - Ventral vagal (calm, connected, safe)
   - Sympathetic (fight-or-flight, anxious, angry)
   - Dorsal vagal (shutdown, disconnected, numb)

Pay attention to how your body felt—were you relaxed, tense, jittery, or shut down?

Step 3: Examine Your Behaviors, Feelings, and Emotions

Now, think about how you responded:

1. What actions did you take? (e.g., did you withdraw, react impulsively, stay calm?)

2. What emotions surfaced? (e.g., anxiety, frustration, joy, hopelessness)

Step 4: Notice the Story or Narrative You Created

Next, consider the narrative you created about the event:

1. What thoughts did you have in response to the situation? (e.g., "They don't care about me," "I'm not good enough," "Everything is going to be fine")
2. How was this story shaped by your nervous system's state? Think about whether the story was shaped by a calm, open state or a more stressed, reactive state.

Step 5: Reframe the Story from a Different State

Now, think about how the story could change if you were in a different state:

1. If you were in a calm (ventral vagal) state, how might you have interpreted the event differently?
2. If you were stressed (fight or flight) or shut down (dorsal vagal), how might that have distorted your perspective?

Understanding how your state affects your narrative can help you create a more balanced story in future situations.

Example:

Event: "I waved to an old colleague at a social event, and they didn't wave back."

Nervous system state: "Immediately, I felt myself slip into a shut down (dorsal vagal) state. My body felt heavy, and I started to feel disconnected, almost numb. My energy drained, and I felt like withdrawing from the event."

Behavior/Feelings: "I stopped interacting with people and found a quiet corner to sit by myself. Emotionally, I felt embarrassed, rejected, and invisible. I avoided eye contact with others and stayed quiet for the rest of the evening."

Story: "The story that formed in my mind was, 'I don't matter to them anymore. I'm not important, and people don't care about me.' This narrative made me feel insignificant and rejected."

Reframing: "If I had been in a ventral vagal state, I might have thought, 'Maybe they didn't see me, or they're distracted. It's nothing personal.' I can see now that my nervous system shut down in response to a perceived rejection, making the situation feel much more painful than it actually was."

This example illustrates how a dorsal vagal (shutdown) state can lead to feelings of disconnection and create stories of rejection and unworthiness. Recognizing how the nervous system influences these narratives can help shift toward a more balanced interpretation.

Step 6: Reflect

Once you've gone through the exercise, take a moment to journal:

- How did your nervous system's state influence your interpretation of the situation?
- What did you learn about the connection between your body's state and the story you told yourself?
- How might you practice shifting your state in the future to reframe your stories?

Recognizing how your body's state affects your perspective can help you become more aware of emotional triggers and respond with greater clarity, even in challenging moments.

CHAPTER 13

Putting it all Together

Nadia's Story

Background and Childhood Experiences

Nadia, age 43, grew up as the youngest of three children in a household marked by chaos and emotional neglect. Her older brother's addiction dominated the family's dynamics, leaving her parents perpetually preoccupied with managing his crises. Her father worked long hours to support the family financially, while her mother oscillated between moments of despair and bursts of frenzied caregiving for her brother. In this tumultuous environment, Nadia felt like an afterthought.

From an early age, Nadia learned to suppress her emotions. Whenever she expressed frustration, fear, or sadness, her parents would tell her, "You're the strong one. We can't deal with this right now." Her feelings were often dismissed as trivial compared to the gravity of her brother's struggles. This reinforced a devastating message: *her needs didn't matter, and she was unimportant.*

A pivotal moment occurred when Nadia was ten years old. After weeks of preparation, she won first place in a school writing competition. She came home excited to share her accomplishment, only to find her parents consumed with worry over her brother's disappearance following another relapse. Her certificate sat unnoticed on the kitchen counter, and no one acknowledged her achievement. In that moment, Nadia's belief solidified: no matter how hard she tried, her efforts and emotions would always take a backseat to the needs of others.

Over time, this belief became a part of Nadia's identity. She stopped voicing her needs, fearing they would be dismissed. She internalized the idea that her worth was tied to how much she could accommodate others, and she learned to silence her own desires to maintain peace in her family.

Self-Sabotaging Behavior in Adulthood

As an adult, Nadia's belief that her needs didn't matter drove patterns of self-sabotaging behavior in both her personal and professional life. Her tendency to prioritize others at the expense of herself left her feeling stuck, unfulfilled, and invisible.

In relationships, Nadia gravitated toward emotionally unavailable partners. She often found herself in one-sided dynamics where she gave endlessly but received little in return. For example, in her twenties she dated a man who frequently canceled plans and dismissed her feelings when she expressed disappointment. Nadia stayed in the relationship for years, rationalizing his behavior and telling herself that expecting more would make her a burden. This pattern repeated itself, reinforcing her belief that she didn't deserve to have her needs met.

Professionally, Nadia excelled at her job but struggled to advocate for herself. She avoided seeking recognition, even when she knew her contributions were significant. During a performance review in her early thirties, her manager praised her work and encouraged her to apply for a leadership role. Nadia deflected the compliment and later convinced herself that she wasn't qualified, allowing the opportunity to pass her by. Her reluctance to pursue advancement stemmed from a deep-seated fear of failure and a belief that she wasn't important enough to be in the spotlight.

In friendships, Nadia's people-pleasing tendencies left her drained. She was the friend everyone relied on for support but rarely reciprocated. When she felt overwhelmed, she kept silent, afraid that setting boundaries would push people away. This pattern of giving without receiving perpetuated her belief that her role was to serve others while her own needs remained unaddressed.

Nadia's Parts: Exiles, Managers, and Firefighters

Through our work together, Nadia began to understand her internal dynamics using the Internal Family Systems (IFS) framework. She identified the key parts of herself that were working in response to her core belief that her needs didn't matter:

- *Exiles (Wounded "Inner Child")*:

Nadia's exiles carried the emotional wounds of her childhood. These parts held the pain of feeling invisible, neglected, and unimportant. They were tied to moments like being ignored after her writing competition win or being told to suppress her emotions for the sake of the family. These parts lived in fear of rejection and carried a profound sense of loneliness.

- *Managers (Proactive Protectors)*:

To shield her exiles from further pain, Nadia's managers developed strategies to keep her safe. These protectors manifested as perfectionism and people-pleasing. By staying agreeable and accommodating, Nadia hoped to avoid conflict and maintain her relationships. Her managers worked hard to convince her that focusing on others was the best way to prevent rejection.

- Firefighters (Reactive Protectors):

When the pain of neglect and invisibility became overwhelming, Nadia's firefighters stepped in to distract her from her emotions. These parts drove her to engage in numbing behaviors like scrolling on her phone for hours or downing a pint of ice cream. While these strategies provided temporary relief, they often left her feeling more disconnected and unfulfilled.

Through therapy, Nadia began to recognize these parts as protective mechanisms that had developed to help her survive her childhood. She learned to approach them with compassion and curiosity, thanking them for their good intentions, and allowing them to take a step back.

Brain and Body: Nadia's Nervous System and Stress Response

Nadia's childhood experiences shaped how her nervous system responded to stress. Growing up in a chaotic environment where her emotional needs were consistently overlooked, Nadia's body learned to adapt in ways that persisted into adulthood:

- Fight-or-Flight:

Nadia's nervous system often became activated in response to perceived rejection or criticism. She would overcompensate, working tirelessly to prove her worth, and avoided situations that required her to assert herself, such as asking for a raise or addressing a partner's dismissive behavior.

- *Shut Down/Collapse*:

When the stress felt overwhelming, Nadia experienced emotional numbness, disengaging from her environment. For example, after a painful breakup, she spent weeks isolating herself, unable to process her emotions or make decisions about her future.

- *Fawn Response:*

Nadia frequently used the fawn response to avoid conflict. She agreed to things she didn't want to do, such as taking on extra work or accommodating a friend's unreasonable demands, in an attempt to keep others happy and maintain a sense of connection.

Recognizing these patterns, Nadia began using tools like mindfulness and grounding exercises to regulate her nervous system. She practiced slowing her breathing during moments of anxiety and used visualization techniques to remind herself that she was safe in the present moment. Over time, these practices helped her shift out of survival mode and respond to stress with greater resilience.

Rewriting Her Narrative: Using Neuroplasticity to Create New Beliefs

Healing required Nadia to challenge her belief that her needs didn't matter. Through the concept of neuroplasticity, she began rewiring her brain to form a new, empowering narrative: "*My needs matter, and I am important.*"

- Recognizing the Old Story:

Nadia became aware of the moments when her old belief surfaced, such as when she hesitated to ask for help or dismissed her own accomplishments. She practiced pausing and asking herself, "Is this belief serving me?"

- Replacing Negative Thoughts:

Through affirmations, reframing, and journaling, Nadia worked to replace her old narrative with a new one. Each morning, she repeated phrases like, "I am worthy of love and care," reinforcing this belief until it became internalized.

- Taking Small Steps:

Nadia started setting boundaries in ways that felt low-risk, such as declining a request to take on extra work when she felt overwhelmed. Each time she prioritized her needs, she built confidence in her ability to advocate for herself and reinforced the belief that she was important and her needs mattered.

The Transformation

Over time, these practices created new neural pathways in Nadia's brain, allowing her to approach life through the lens of empowerment rather than unworthiness. Internally, Nadia experienced a deep shift. The pervasive feeling of being unimportant no longer controlled her decisions. By rewriting her core belief, she embraced a future where her needs mattered just as much as anyone else's. Through her journey, Nadia found the courage to live authentically, with confidence and self-worth.

Final Discovery Prompt: Rewriting Your Narrative and Building a New Belief System

This final exercise is about taking those old beliefs you've identified throughout this book and rewriting them into a new, empowering narrative that reflects who you want to be. Cognitive Behavioral Therapy (CBT) shows us that our thoughts, beliefs, and behaviors are all intertwined. By challenging outdated beliefs, you will also shift how you think, feel, and act. Reference the example below before you get started.

Step 1: Your Current Story – Old Beliefs and Patterns

Start by taking the beliefs and behaviors that have shaped your life so far. Fill in the sections below:

How it is now:

- Briefly describe how you feel your life is currently—how you act, think, and respond.

My current beliefs:

- *I am...* (What negative beliefs do you hold about yourself?)
- *People are...* (What negative beliefs do you hold about others?)
- *The world is...* (What limiting beliefs do you hold about life or the world?)

My current rules that protect me:

- *If... then...* (What mental rules have you created to avoid harm? These are often rigid, fear-based rules.)

My current coping strategies:

- What self-sabotaging behaviors do you engage in to cope or protect yourself?

Step 2: Your New Story – Creating Empowering Beliefs and Behaviors

Now, let's rewrite the script. This is where you define a new, positive belief system that reflects your true self. Speak in the present tense as though this is already your reality.

How I'd like it to be:

- Describe how you think, feel, and act, focusing on the version of yourself that you are aspiring to be.

My new beliefs:

- *I am...* (What empowering/compassionate beliefs do you hold about yourself?)
- *People are...* (What healthier/positive beliefs do you hold about others?)
- *The world is...* (What healthier/positive beliefs do you hold about life or the world?)

My new rules that protect me:

- *If... then...* (What flexible, growth-oriented rules can you set for yourself that support well-being?)

My new strategies:

- What healthy behaviors and coping skills will you adopt to support this new belief system?

This exercise allows you to identify the limiting beliefs and behaviors that hold you back, and create a healthier mindset and more adaptive coping strategies. By reflecting on how you'd like to be, you can begin to shift toward a new narrative that promotes growth, connection, and self-worth.

Repeating the New Narrative to Make It Stick

The key to rewiring your brain is consistency. Repetition is how your subconscious learns, so repeat these new beliefs and this narrative to yourself *multiple times per day* as though it's *already true* and *already happening*. The more you affirm these new beliefs, the more your mind starts to internalize them as being factual. Just like with any habit, the more you practice, the more natural it becomes. Keep reminding yourself of this new version of you until it feels real—because it *is* real, it's just been overpowered by your subconscious for a long time.

Example:

Current Story (Old System):

How it felt:

"I constantly feel anxious about not doing things perfectly. I'm paralyzed by the fear of making mistakes and often procrastinate or avoid tasks altogether. Nothing ever feels good enough, no matter how hard I try."

My old beliefs:

- I am... "I'm never good enough unless I'm perfect."
- People are... "People only value me if I perform up to their standards."

- The world is... "The world is a place where mistakes are judged harshly."

My old rules that protect me:

- If I don't start a task, then I can't fail at it.
- If I strive for perfection, then I can avoid criticism.

My old coping strategies:

- Procrastinating, overthinking, avoiding risks, constantly revising or redoing work.

New Story (New System):

How I feel:

"I take action with confidence and embrace imperfection as a natural part of growth. I trust my best effort is enough and focus on progress, not perfection."

My new beliefs:

- I am... "I am enough as I am, even when I make mistakes."
- People are... "People value me for who I am, not just for what I can do or achieve."
- Life is... "Life is a setting for learning and growing, not for being perfect. All humans are imperfect and vulnerable at times."

My new rules that protect me:

- If I take small, imperfect steps, then I will make progress and learn.
- If I allow myself to make mistakes, then I'll grow and develop resilience to feeling disappointed or embarrassed.

CHAPTER 14

Wrapping Up:
What Comes Next?

So, what's your story? As we come to the end of this book, I hope that everything we've worked through together has left you feeling seen, validated, and empowered. My goal was to create an opportunity for you to explore your own experiences and realize that the struggles you face aren't a reflection of your competence or worth, but often the result of deeply ingrained core beliefs from childhood. These beliefs, while initially formed to protect you, have likely continued shaping your thoughts, feelings, and actions in ways that don't serve you now. The good news is, with self-awareness and reflection, you have the power to rewrite the story you've been telling yourself.

Let's take a moment to reflect on what we've covered. Early on, we talked about how everyone sees the world through their own unique lens, shaped by core beliefs—like a pair of sunglasses that colors your view of everything. Maybe your "shades" are tinted by self-doubt, fear of rejection, or the need to be perfect. These beliefs, though deeply ingrained, are not facts. Recognizing that they're conditioned responses rather than hard truths is the first step in loosening their grip on your life.

We also dove into how these beliefs are formed, often in childhood. Whether through direct experiences like criticism or neglect, or more subtle messages like feeling unimportant or unseen, these experiences shape the beliefs you carry with you—beliefs like "I'm not good enough" or "I have to be perfect to be loved." No one has a perfect childhood, and we all end up carrying beliefs that may have protected us back then but no longer serve us now. The best part? Just as these beliefs were formed, they can be transformed. By recognizing how they show up in your life today, you can start shifting them to align with the person you're working toward becoming.

In the later chapters, we explored how these beliefs manifest as self-sabotaging behaviors. Whether it's procrastination, perfectionism, imposter syndrome, or overworking, these behaviors are often unconscious attempts to protect ourselves from perceived threats like rejection, failure, or criticism. But instead of protecting us, they hold us back. The key is to identify the behaviors and trace them back to their root beliefs. It's not about willpower or trying harder—it's about understanding why you act the way you do and offering yourself compassion as you work toward change.

One of the biggest takeaways from this book is that healing starts with awareness. You can't change what you don't first acknowledge and accept. Once you start recognizing the core beliefs that drive your behaviors, you can begin to make conscious choices that align with who you truly are, not who you were conditioned to be. Whether it's the belief that you need to be perfect to be loved or that your worth is tied to pleasing others, these beliefs can be questioned and reshaped.

And as you do the work, you'll start to feel a shift—not just in your behavior, but in how you see yourself.

We also talked about how your nervous system plays a huge role in shaping your emotional responses. Polyvagal Theory showed us how our body's stress responses are tied to our past experiences, and how our nervous system influences the stories we tell ourselves about what's happening. By learning to recognize when your body is in survival mode, you can begin to separate the physical state from the narrative your mind creates. This awareness helps you shift back to a place of safety and connection when those old stories resurface.

But understanding all this is just the first step. True transformation happens when you put these insights into practice—when you start trusting yourself, your needs, and your inner wisdom. Trusting yourself means letting go of the need to control everything, predict the future, or seek validation from others. When you trust yourself, you no longer need to prove your worth because you already know you're worthy.

Self-compassion has been another big theme throughout this book. It's not a luxury; it's essential. That harsh inner critic many of us carry is often rooted in the very core beliefs we're trying to unlearn. Learning to be kind to yourself, even when you make mistakes or fall short, is a critical part of healing. Self-compassion lets you accept your humanness and remember that you are deserving of love and respect, flaws and all.

Suffering, failure, and imperfection are part of what it means to be human—a universal thread that connects us all. These challenges, though often tangled up with feelings of shame or inadequacy, aren't signs of personal failure. They're simply reflections of the human experience. Kristin Neff, a pioneer in self-compassion research, reminds us that recognizing this truth can help us shift from self-judgment to self-kindness. Instead of seeing imperfection as a flaw to fix, it becomes a bridge—an opportunity to connect with others, learn from hardship, and embrace life in all its messy fullness. This mindset fosters resilience and emotional well-being, reminding us that being human means facing both joy and struggle with compassion and courage.

We also touched on the importance of letting go of blame—not for the sake of the other person, but for ourselves. It's not about excusing what they did or letting them off the hook. Instead, it's about recognizing how *our perception* of their actions contributed to the formation of our core beliefs. The way we interpreted their behavior shaped the stories we've carried, and while we can't change what happened, we can choose how we move forward. Forgiveness in this context is really for us. It allows us to release the resentment or anger we've been holding onto, which only serves to give them continued control over our emotions and beliefs. By choosing to forgive, we reclaim our power, no longer letting past hurts dictate how we feel or who we are today. This act of forgiveness doesn't change the past—it changes *our relationship* with it.

As we close out this experience together, I hope you feel more connected to yourself. You now have the tools to recognize the core beliefs that have been holding you back—and more importantly, you have the ability to change them. It won't happen overnight, and it will take ongoing effort, but it's worth it. Imagine living without the constant fear of rejection, without needing to be perfect, and without questioning your worth. That life is possible, and it starts with the work you've already begun.

Remember, you are not defined by your past or the beliefs you've carried with you. You are capable of growth, healing, and transformation. Wherever you are on your path, you are worthy of love, value, and respect. Trust in yourself and trust in the process. The more you believe in your own worth, the less you'll need to control, predict, or seek approval. With that trust comes a sense of freedom that allows you to face whatever comes your way with grace and confidence.

Thank you for trusting me to take you on this little adventure of self-awareness and introspection. I hope this book has given you the insight and tools to move forward with more self-compassion, internal validation, and a deeper sense of self-worth.

I now channel everything I've learned and experienced into helping others understand and overcome the patterns that hold them back. I provide both individual and group coaching, guiding people through the same struggles I once faced. I also speak professionally for organizations and corporations, bringing psychological insight to a broader audience. And because I believe this work should be accessible to everyone, I share a wealth of free content on my social media channels—so whether you're in a session, at a keynote, or just scrolling, you'll always find something to challenge the way you think. All of my information can be found here: https://bio.site/kristenjacobsen

I'm also giving you a sneak peek at the workbook that accompanies this book—starting with the first exercise, completely FREE. If you found the discovery prompts in these pages helpful, the workbook takes it even further, guiding you through deeper exercises designed to create real, lasting change. Scan the QR code below to grab your freebie!

I'll leave you with one of my favorite affirmations. Repeat it to yourself with compassion whenever you're feeling inadequate:

"I'm just human, doing the best I can, under these circumstances, with the resources I have available to me."

REFERENCES

Amen Clinics. (2024, August 5). *Negative thinking: Do you have an ANT infestation in your head?* Amen Clinics. https://www.amenclinics.com/blog/negative-thinking-do-you-have-an-ant-infestation-in-your-head/

Beck, A. T., Rush, A. J., Shaw, B. F., & Emery, G. (2024). *Cognitive therapy of depression* (2nd ed.). Guilford Press.

Dana, D. (2018). *The polyvagal theory in therapy: Engaging the rhythm of regulation.* W. W. Norton & Company.

Dweck, C. S. (2006). *Mindset: The new psychology of success.* Random House.Dweck, C. S. (2006). *Mindset: The new psychology of success.* Random House.

EMDR Consulting. (2021). *EMDR training course: Belief-focused approach.* Roy Kiessling, LISW (Founder/CEO). EMDR Consulting.

EMDR International Association. (n.d.). *EMDRIA: Eye Movement Desensitization and Reprocessing therapy.* Retrieved November 27, 2024, from https://www.emdria.org

Erikson, E. H. (1963). *Childhood and society* (2nd ed.). W. W. Norton & Company.

Gibson, L. C. (2015). *Adult children of emotionally immature parents: How to heal from distant, rejecting, or self-involved parents.* New Harbinger Publications.

Kay, K., & Shipman, C. (2014, May). The confidence gap: Evidence shows that women are less self-assured than men—and that to succeed, confidence matters as much as competence. *The Atlantic*. https://www.theatlantic.com/magazine/archive/2014/05/the-confidence-gap/359815/

Markus, H. (1977). Self-schemata and processing information about the self. *Journal of Personality and Social Psychology, 35*(2), 63–78.

Molinsky, A. (2016, July 7). Everyone suffers from impostor syndrome — here's how to handle it. *Harvard Business Review*. https://hbr.org/2016/07/everyone-suffers-from-impostor-syndrome-heres-how-to-handle-it

Orbé-Austin, L., & Orbé-Austin, R. (2020). Own your greatness: Overcome imposter syndrome, beat self-doubt, and succeed in life. Ulysses Press.

Porges, S. W. (2011). *The polyvagal theory: Neurophysiological foundations of emotions, attachment, communication, and self-regulation*. W. W. Norton & Company.

Schwartz, R. C. (2021). *No bad parts: Healing trauma and restoring wholeness with the Internal Family Systems model*. Sounds True.

Shapiro, F. (1987). Eye movement desensitization: A new treatment for post-traumatic stress disorder. *Journal of Behavior Therapy and Experimental Psychiatry, 18*(3), 211–217.

Tulshyan, R., & Burey, J.-A. (2021, February 11). Stop telling women they have imposter syndrome: For many women, feeling like an outsider isn't an illusion — it's the result of systemic bias and exclusion. Harvard Business Review. https://hbr.org/2021/02/stop-telling-women-they-have-imposter-syndrome

www.ingramcontent.com/pod-product-compliance
Lightning Source LLC
Chambersburg PA
CBHW071727120626
46550CB00002B/420